Let's talk about Politics & Religion

Let's talk about Politics & Religion

T.G. Vitko

Columbus, Ohio

Let's talk about Politics & Religion

Published by Gatekeeper Press
2167 Stringtown Rd, Suite 109
Columbus, OH 43123-2989
www.GatekeeperPress.com

The cover design for this book is entirely the product of the author. Gatekeeper Press did not participate in and is not responsible for any aspect of this element.

Library of Congress Control Number: 2021938899

ISBN (paperback): 9781662914454

Let's Talk about Politics and Religion

It is said that politics is the art of government, that is, the exercise of control over the people through the making and enforcement of collective decisions. That control provides politicians the power to influence our actions, beliefs, and/or behaviors unless we the people set the limits to that influence. Similarly, religion is a set of beliefs and practices based on faith (believing in something even if you cannot see it) that serve to subordinate us to something superior or holy in order to explain the extraordinary mystery of life that surround us. The same life that science attempts at describing but cannot fully explain. Religions are managed by people who also exercise control over the people through the making and enforcement of canonical decisions borne from ancestral beliefs and traditions.

Looking at the countries of the world, we see enormous differences. Among the countries with large amounts of natural resources, some thrive, and others struggle. Of the countries with few natural resources, again some thrive, and others struggle. What makes some countries prosperous and other countries unsuccessful? Without any doubt, the cause of such differences is the people in power, both in political and religious affairs, which control the fate of their people.

This book analyzes the various schools of thought, both political and religious, puts them through a logical analysis of the facts, and answers the following questions: Which are the most beneficial political systems for the majority of people? Which political system has failed every time it has been tried? Why is there a separation of church and state? Is it possible to discuss religion? If there is one God, why are there so many religions? Which are the religious writings that claim to be of God? Are we able to discern among these writings which one is true? What is truth? What does the true Word of God really say? What does the Word of God say about our history and our future?

All very challenging questions that most are afraid to ask or that think these have no answers. This book attempts to provide answers to these questions through a rational and conscientious process based on facts.

Introduction

People often say: "Let's not talk about politics or religion" as a way to avoid conflict. Those people only feel comfortable talking about what naturally is left out: small talk and gossip. Both these discourse types do not need much thought behind the words; they are simply unconstructive and often destructive.

The truth is that politics and religion (better said, God) are the two paramount subjects that all people should have an opinion about. Why? Because politics rules our physical being and God rules our spiritual being. One deals with the life we live now, and the other about the life we will live eternally. If that is not important to you, I do not know what is.

So, why is it that people do not want to talk about these seemingly important subjects? Simply said, because talking about these require a degree of knowledge about an ample range of subjects. Most people do not want to bother taking the time to read, think, and discuss in order to cultivate an opinion based on facts about politics and religion, so they choose the easy way out: avoidance and indifference. It denotes the poor level of education schools provide lately. In the past, high schools had compulsory classes on philosophy, economics, civics, and religion. These courses provided, unlike other classes, ample room for discussing different points of view among the students and the teachers. To this day, I remember the back and forth arguments, which often continued outside the classroom on "does the means justify the end?" or "when does the life of a fetus really begin?" among others.

To talk about politics requires a basic knowledge of philosophy (different schools of thought, how they came to be, and the basis for each), of history (different socio-economic models tried over time and the outcomes of each), of psychology (how human nature adapted or reacted to the different schools of though and to the different socio-economic models), of practicality (if they succeeded in making life better for people in different socio-economic levels of society), and finally a lot of common sense and logic to marry all these seemingly complicated aspects with our own life experiences and the historical facts.

To talk about religion requires some knowledge of the major religions. It is important to know a bit about the origins, beliefs, and doctrines of each religion, especially those religions whose writings claim to be of God. With that background, your arguments will be solid, and your faith in your own beliefs will be reinforced. For those who consider themselves agnostic or atheistic, there is a section in the book that discusses with detail this position as well.

The more you know about the above-mentioned subjects, the more "academic" you will sound while discussing them with people. However, a basic knowledge about these subjects is enough to form in you a firm position based on concepts that are fairly clear to everyone who approaches it in an unbiased and tolerant manner. This is key, and this is true with any learning experience: it is necessary to approach it with an open mind. It is impossible to learn new concepts with a mind made up. It is crucial to consider and ponder about new concepts and facts as presented. It is impossible to learn while trying to measure it against a personal judgment biased point of view. But the opposite is also true; if enough proof exists demonstrating an idea is true, it is essential to accept it as a fact, build upon that fact and move on to the next concept or idea.

Another aspect that is also absolutely true about any learning experience: this is an exercise of pure logic. It is necessary to leave feelings about things aside. I realize this is difficult for some people to do, especially in today's age of "everything is about feelings." People no longer say, "I think this or that" but "I feel this or that." It is OK to have feelings, but a sign of maturity is the ability to know when it is the time to listen to your heart and when to allow your brain to take over and deal with issues with logic.

It is natural for youngsters to question everything, especially about those things that are clearly wrong with society. Maturity teaches you to find the root cause of the issues instead of simply reacting emotionally about the injustices of this world. Maybe that is the reason many people do not try to think deeper about things. But we have been created with a mind and a heart. A heart to feel compassion and love, and a mind to regulate, to draw from experience, to discern what is good and what is better, given the circumstances. Let us not keep our minds idle and governed by feelings. If you believe strongly about something, don't just feel compassion, caring, love, hate, or disgust, but think what can be done to resolve it. Feelings exist to get your brain working. Once your being goes from feeling to working, it is time to research the issue thoroughly and follow it with actions. Feelings are fleeting. They change with our circumstance. Ideas, on the other hand, remain and build upon each other, forming concepts that become irrefutable. There is a reason why our brains are on top of our heart. Our mind was meant to rule over our heart!

Talking About Politics

Political ideologies go hand in hand with philosophical schools of thought. The study of philosophy is divided into:

- Aesthetics that studies the nature of beauty, art, and taste, and the creation of personal kinds of truths.
- Epistemology that studies the source, nature, and validity of knowledge. Things like: How is knowledge different from belief? How much can we know? How does knowledge come about? Can knowledge be objective?
- Ethics that studies what is right, what is good, and what is valuable. It attempts to use philosophical methods to identify the morally correct course of action in various fields of human life.

There are many philosophical schools of thought. The major schools of philosophical thought have evolved over time, building upon the ideas of previous schools, which are presented here with a summary in chronological order:

1. Early Naturalists: 600-400 BC, Thales de Miletus, Heraclitus, Democritus

What is the true hidden nature of reality? Is it one of the simple ingredients of the visible world, such as air, earth, fire, or water? Or hidden tiny simple units called 'atoms'? We can explain things without reference to the gods. Reality is simple.

2. Buddhism: 600-500 BC, Gautama Buddha

Suffering has a cause, and we can overcome it by means of meditation, following the noble eightfold path, and contemplation of sutras. The many schools of Buddhism are rather diverse in their thought, bound together primarily by the Buddha's ideas on suffering. Truth is in suffering.

3. Early Rationalists: 510-430 BC, Pythagoras, Parmenides, Zeno

If reason and appearances disagree, which one should we believe? Since reality is hidden, reason is more reliable. Math is the key. We can deduce the existence of some very simple, single, and pure reality. Reality is in ideas.

4. Athenian Sophists: 450-400 BC, Protagoras, Gorgias

If people make judgments, doesn't morality and truth depend on the observer, and therefore they do not exist in reality? Relativism is indeed true, so morality is invented for our own (selfish) convenience, and neither our sense nor our reason can be trusted. Ideals are false.

5. Socrates and his followers: 430-370 BC, Socrates

Can we avoid the dangers of relativism, which seems to undermine morality and make the pursuit of truth impossible? Although both senses and reason are riddled with doubts, right thinking will lead to truth, and moral goodness will naturally follow from a perception of the truth. Doubt leads to goodness.

6. Platonic Academy: 390-270 BC, Plato

Must we not be committed to some more eternal and unchanging ideals if we are going to be committed to goodness and truth? Reason shows us that there must be a set of fixed and unchanging ideas, which not only explain our highest ideals, but also the ordinary way we understand concepts and language. Follow ideals.

7. Aristotle and the Peripatetics: 350-270 BC, Aristotle

Can we not get a clear grip on knowledge and goodness without being committed to some unrealistic ideals which we cannot experience? The essence of the things we experience are eternal and unchanging so that we can come to understand the truth, purpose, and virtue of each thing by a careful combination of observation and analysis. Analyze the essence of each thing.

8. Skeptics: 350-250 BC, Pyrrho

Are not the doubts raised by philosophy so overwhelming and contradictory that it makes all confident judgment impossible? For every argument invented, there seems to be a plausible counter-argument, so the best solution is just to become very passive, which brings great peace of mind. Become passive.

9. Cynics: 390-300 BC, Diogenes

Once it becomes clear that morality and customs are invented by humans, why should a rational person conform to them? We should abandon conventional rules and follow our own personal desires, though experience shows that the best life is not self-indulgent but quite simple and restrained. Do your own thing.

10. Epicureans (Hedonism): 310-250 BC, Epicurus, Lucretius

If the naturalists are right in their explanations of reality, what implications has this for how we should live our lives? The naturalists do seem to give the best explanations of existence, so we should accept their reliance on the senses and their belief in atoms? The best life is, therefore, the one that brings happiness for us as physical creatures, which is a life of cautious pleasure. Pursue quiet pleasure.

11. Stoics: 300-200 BC Zeno of Citium, Chrysippus

Can we not find some balanced combination of the extreme doctrines and then deduce a correct way of living? Knowledge must come from a combination of senses and reason. We must accept the material world, as it is designed and guided by gods. We must therefore live in accordance with nature and learn a quiet acceptance of even the cruelest natural events. Show restraint.

12. Neo-Platonists: AD 230-350, Plotinus

How far can reason go in deducing the true nature of reality behind the world of physical appearances? We can now see that Plato's forms are religious in character and exist eternally in the mind of God. The form of pure goodness sought by Plato is the same as God himself. Dream of the high ideals.

13. Christians: AD 150-1400, Augustine, Aquinas

What are the logical implications of Christ's teachings, and are they compatible with the teachings of the pagan philosophers? Although Aristotle and Plato lacked Christian revelation, their ideas on metaphysics, politics, virtue, and logic fit well with Christianity and greatly extend it as an intellectual theory. Christian problems like free will and the existence of evil need the help of pagan philosophers. Follow Christ rationally.

14. Islamic Aristotelians: AD 900-1100, Averroes, Avicenna

How far can the ideas of Aristotle be fitted into the teachings of Mohammed in the Koran? Islam is an all-embracing religion, which should try to incorporate the obvious wisdom gained by the pagan philosophers into its own view of reality. Islam is rational.

15. Empiricists: 1690-1770, Locke, Berkeley, Hume

Given that sensorial experience is our only source of knowledge, how far can knowledge extend, and what are the inevitable limitations? We can see that science is the best route to truth, and philosophy shows us the limitations of claims about perception, knowledge, truth, laws, causation, the future, morality, and politics when they are built up purely from basic sensorial experiences. Be scientific.

16. Rationalists: 1640-1800, Descartes, Spinoza, Leibniz, Kant

Given that reason is our only reliable source of knowledge, what can we deduce about reality from pure thought, and how far can we trust the appearances of sensorial experience? Reason tells us to mistrust our senses, but ideas and truth exist within the mind, and by careful thought, we can build a picture of reality using reason, mathematics, and intuition. Science has its place within a larger spiritual and intellectual world. Follow reason in everything.

17. Idealists: 1800-1900, Hegel

If we take a commitment to rationalism seriously, what can we deduce about the true nature and purposes of existence? If we follow our reason far enough, we can see all ideas (and even history itself) converging on a single ideal and a single vision of the truth, which exists in a spiritual world. Great ideas are reality.

18. Materialists (Marxism): 1600-1900, Hobbes, Marx, Darwin

Given that the only thing existing in our world is physical matter, what can we deduce about our identity, and how should individuals and communities live their lives? If we start with our senses, we realize that nothing is sure except the physical world, so we must assume that nothing else exists, either inside our own heads or in any greater world of the spirit. The laws of science are the laws of human life. Stick to what is physical.

19. Phenomenologists: 1870-1930, Husserl, Merleau-Ponty, Sartre, Heidegger

If Kant has shown that knowledge depends on how our minds work, can we sometimes still get at the truth? By analyzing our own minds, we should be able to gradually strip away any distortions and distinguish reality from appearances. Analyze the mind.

20. Existentialists: 1850-1950, Kierkegaard, Nietzsche, Sartre

If we accept our feeling of mental freedom as being true, how should we exercise this responsibility in our lives? We must understand that we cannot only escape social pressures but also mental pressures. We are responsible for everything we do and everything we are. Live through decisions.

21. Logical Analysts: 1880-1980, Frege, Russell, Moore, Ayer

If problems are broken down into steps and attention paid to precise logic and evidence (like science), can we reach the truth? While a cautious approach makes big metaphysical claims look very doubtful, we can make progress, especially in understanding the complex role which language and the nature of the mind play in our own thinking. Analyze problems into parts.

22. Romanticists: 1900s, Hegel, Schelling, and Fichte

Emphasize emotional self-awareness as a necessary precondition to improving society and bettering the human condition. Be self-aware.

23. Pragmatists: 1880-1980, Peirce, James, Quine

Can we bring philosophy closer to how normal people acquire knowledge and make decisions? We actually accept things are true because they work in practice, and this rule can be the basis for morality and politics, as well as scientific knowledge. Follow what succeeds.

24. Post-Modernists: 1970-1990, Derrida

What follows from the fact that relativism is right, and truth and morality change continually with culture and prejudice? Nothing is objectively true, and even language is beyond our control, so we must just 'go with the flow' and not expect any kind of stable truth or science or morality or politics. Relax.

25. Structuralists: 1900s, Lévi-Strauss

Human culture, being a set of learned behaviors and ideas that characterize a society, is just an expression of the underlying structures of the human mind. Re-structure.

Analysis of Philosophical Movements

Now that you have been presented with all the available philosophical movements, it is normal to agree with several different ones. One notable philosophy missing in this list is Monotheism, which dates back to 2100 BC with Abraham, which predates Early Naturalists by 1,500 years! It may not be considered a philosophy by scholars because the idea claims to come directly from God. However, Abraham is considered the father of the Jewish (and by consequence, the Christian) and of the Muslim religions. This is a huge oversight in academic references.

What amazes me is that the Early Naturalists, as far back as 600 BC, already had developed a concept of unity of matter, the atom, but fell in the trap of trying to explain it all in the absence of God. This is exactly how many people think nowadays. Many say: "I believe in science" as a way to discard everything supernatural, but believe in, for example, fluid sexuality when science clearly states that men have XY chromosomes and women XX chromosomes. Not a good argument for evolution. It looks more like we are returning back to the Early Naturalists in a vicious cycle.

We have gone from reality is simple, to truth is in suffering, to reality is in ideas, to ideals are false, to doubt leads to goodness, to follow ideals, to analyze the essence of each thing, to become passive, to do your own thing, to pursue quiet pleasure, to show restraint, to dream of the high ideals, to follow Christ rationally, to Islam is rational, to be scientific, to follow reason in everything, to great ideas are reality, to stick to what is physical, to analyze the mind, to live through decisions, to analyze problems into parts, to follow what succeeds, to relax, to re-structure, and to be self-aware.

Looking at it in this fast-forward way, it appears to describe the stages in life of a very troubled person. The good thing is that most people could care less about what the philosophers across ages were thinking about and what philosophical movements they came out with. Most people were too busy working and fighting to stay alive. Philosophy was mostly a preoccupation of the ruling classes. The advantage humanity had in the past that shielded most of the population from these ideological movements was poor communication. This does not mean that some philosophies did not have a meaningful and wide impact in different cultures of the globe at different times in our history. They did, but all of these wide-range philosophical movements, for the most part, were associated with religions. This is true except for the communist and socialist movements in the early 1900s with the caveat that they try to replace religion with the cult of the State.

Monotheism, introduced very early in human history (2100 BC), did not have a global impact in the western part of the world until after 300 years of Christian persecution, torture, and killings that ensued after the death of Jesus. Islam makes its appearance in the Arab region only 300 years after Christianity was adopted by the Romans as their religion. In the eastern part of the world, Buddhism expands with a non-theistic religion. The Buddha himself rejected the idea of a creator god, and Buddhist philosophers have even argued that belief in an eternal god is nothing but a distraction for humans seeking enlightenment.

Communication Crisis

Today the communication insulation described above has been lost with the advent of cell phones, 24-hour news shows, and the Internet with its numerous social media platforms. These platforms that were initially created by the techies to help people get mutually in touch and informed are now exerting their power by blocking certain people from expressing themselves when the ideas some people are trying to express are contrary to the techies' particular ideology. Worse than that, the press and the techies, now converted in Big Tech, are also disseminating false information to confuse or steer people toward a certain ideology. This is causing tension in people, creating polarization. This polarization is caused by the obvious oligopoly of information and the trampling of the First Amendment that protects freedom of expression.

The mainstream press, which was discovered to be in great majority secretly in support of the Democrats even back in the 1990s, at least made then the effort to hide their bias in the news and commentaries. Since they were outed mainly by conservative radio talk shows which became increasingly popular since then, the reaction by the press was not to correct their ways but to openly become the activist for the Democrats, increasingly losing credibility and, by consequence, viewership and readership. According to Gallup, about 60% of people in the 1990s thought the mainstream media reported the news fully, accurately, and fairly. Today it is down to 40%, and over 80% of people believe the mainstream press is biased. We can say that these days journalism is almost dead. Currently, the mainstream media is blatantly the propaganda arm of the Democratic party. Only communist and socialist countries have a press that acts in this manner.

Universities that were once bastions of freedom of speech, notably in the 1960s, are now taken over by socialist zealots. But these socialists are not talking about working-class exploitation and freedom of expression against government-led wars; they have a new narrative: identity socialism. In identity socialism, every minority group in society is a victim of something. They are victims of morality (especially Christian morality), victims of Capitalism, victims of race, victims of culture, even victims of history. This victimhood mentality naturally leads to the idea that certain groups succeeded because they were privileged.

Identity socialists are zealots because they do not allow their narrative to be questioned. Like good zealots, they have become terrorists, as they are trying to muzzle anyone that dissents with their ideas, and when they do not suceed with threats, they resort to violence and destruction. Blatant examples of this behavior are the anarchist Antifa and the communist Black Lives Matter[1] movements. This is the outcome of nonrestrictive parenting, biased teachers and professors, a liberal society, and having too much time and money on their hands. What kind of professionals are the graduates of these schools going to become? Schools are supposed to be safe places to discuss all kinds of ideas, concepts, hypotheses, and theories. Without this discussion, there can be no learning. Schools have become indoctrination camps. What a shame!

1   In 2016, the "Movement for Black Lives," a BLM umbrella organization, released a political platform which consisted of numerous far-left policy proposals, including socialized medicine, the immediate legalization of prostitution, the immediate pardon of all drug offenses with reparations paid to those convicted of drug offenses, and the restructuring of tax policy to create a "radical and sustainable redistribution of wealth."

Political Schools of Thought

Of all the philosophical movements already mentioned, only a few were applied to politics. Politics is broadly seen as the study of government, institutions, and decision-making processes that govern the world we live in. It can also be the study of ideas like justice, democracy, equality, and freedom, and how power is distributed and exercised. Furthermore, the source of power determines the difference between democracies, oligarchies, and autocracies.

In a democracy, political legitimacy is based on popular sovereignty. Forms of democracy include representative democracy (by elected representatives), direct democracy (by referenda), and demarchic (by citizen juries). Democracies can be either republics or constitutional monarchies.

Oligarchy is a power structure where a minority rules. These may be in the form of anocracy (a regime that mixes democratic with autocratic features), aristocracy (a form of government that places strength in the hands of a small, privileged ruling class), ergatocracy (a type of government dominated by the labor and solidarities similar to communist beliefs), geniocracy (advocates a certain minimal criterion of intelligence for political candidates and also of the electorate), gerontocracy (ruled by leaders who are significantly older than most of the adult population), kakistocracy (run by the worst, least qualified, and/or most unscrupulous citizens), kleptocracy (a government whose corrupt leaders use political power to appropriate the wealth of their nation), meritocracy (power is vested to individuals on the basis of talent, effort, and achievement, rather than wealth or social class), noocracy (decision making is in the hands of philosophers), particracy (the political parties are the primary basis of rule rather than citizens and/or individual politicians), plutocracy (a society that is ruled or controlled by people of great wealth or income), stratocracy (government is headed by military chiefs), technocracy (rulers are elected by the population or appointed on the basis of their expertise in a given area of responsibility, particularly with regard to scientific or technical knowledge), theocracy (a deity is recognized as the supreme ruling authority, giving divine guidance to human intermediaries that manage the day-to-day affairs of the government), or timocracy (form of government where only property owners may participate in government).

Autocracies are either dictatorships (including military dictatorships) or absolute monarchies.

A Note on Fascism

Fascism is a form of authoritarian ultranationalism characterized by dictatorial power, forcible suppression of opposition, and strong regimentation of society and of the economy, which came to prominence in the early 1900s. Italy and Germany (and to a lesser degree Spain) formed an Axis in Europe, which initiated World War II against the Allied forces of the United Kingdom, the United States, and the USSR.

The press associates Fascism with the ultra-right. However, the term Nazi comes from the shortening of its proper name in German, "Nationale Sozialist." As its own name says it, it is a socialist movement which is not even close to the far-right ideology that believes in small government, individual freedom, and the power of the Free Market. What does a Nazi socialist organization stand for? A central government taking total control of society, only the governing elite having access to everything while the people are put into the category of useful idiots, kept that way by their "fake news" propaganda office. Once someone becomes a threat to the government, it no longer is useful, and as a result, it is destroyed. Nazis are identical to Communists, except for their racist traits against Jews and other minorities. The only reason Nazis and Communists were enemies in WWII was because they existed at the same historical time and had similar imperialistic ambitions, not because they had a different ideology.

Practical Applications of Political Philosophies

The following are the political schools of thought with practical application in specific countries:

Communism: advocates class war and leads to a society in which all property is publicly owned, and each person works and is paid according to their abilities and needs. They do not believe in democracy and take over power by force. Plato, Marx, Engels, Fourier.

Currently, China, Cuba, and Vietnam are examples of communist countries.

Socialism: believes that the means of production, distribution, and exchange of goods should be owned or regulated by the state. Today it is presented as the intermediate point between Capitalism and Communism, but it is clearly characterized by the dictatorship of the working class. They believe in democracy as a means to acquire power, but once attained, they change the system to perpetuate themselves in power. Marx, Proudhon.

Currently, Algeria, Bangladesh, India, and Nicaragua, are examples of socialist countries.

Liberalism: economically, modern Liberalism opposes cuts to the social safety net and supports a role for government in reducing inequality, providing education, ensuring access to healthcare, regulating economic activity, and protecting the natural environment. Politically, modern Liberalism combines ideas of civil liberty and equality with support for social justice and a mixed economy. In the most part, they believe in democracy but are increasingly becoming staunch supporters of global socialism. Rawls, Locke, Montesquieu.

Currently, Australia, Canada, Sweden, and New Zealand are examples of modern economic liberal countries.

Libertarianism: a laissez-faire political philosophy advocating only minimal state intervention in the lives of citizens. Advocates the demise of the state for the benefit of cooperation between free individuals. They believe in democracy but are currently lured by global socialism. Nozick.

Currently, United Kingdom, Portugal, United States, and Uruguay are examples of libertarian countries.

Free Market: is one where voluntary exchange and the laws of supply and demand provide the sole basis for the economic system, without (or very little) government intervention. A key feature of Free Markets is the absence of coerced or forced transactions or conditions on transactions. They believe in a democracy; however, Hong Kong, since its transfer from the British government to China in 1997, has been experiencing growing pressure on their political autonomy. Adam Smith.

Currently, Hong Kong and Singapore are examples of free-market countries.

Analysis of Political Schools of Thought

The simplest way to tell which political philosophy works best is by analyzing the improvement in wealth of the populace, the protection of citizen's liberties, and the desire of other people to immigrate to that country.

A country's wealth can be measured by the Consumer Price Index (CPI), the per capita Gross Domestic Product (GDP), and the Percent Unemployment.

Inflation - CPI is the variation in prices paid by typical consumers for retail goods and other items (referred to as a basket of goods). It basically measures the country's inflation for the consumers with respect to a base year when CPI equals 100. The greater the inflation, the less acquisition power for that country's currency. In other words, with more inflation, things become more and more expensive to buy.

The basket of goods includes basic food and beverages such as cereal, milk, and coffee. It also includes housing costs, bedroom furniture, apparel, transportation expenses, medical care costs, recreational expenses, toys, and the cost of admissions to museums. Education and communication expenses are included in the basket's contents, as well as other random items such as tobacco, haircuts, and funerals. In the United States, the basket of goods primarily considers purchases made by urban consumers.

The International Monetary Fund (IMF) assumes the responsibility for collecting and reporting of CPI data for a great number of countries around the globe. From the Figure, it is clear that not all countries participate. Many important countries in Europe (Poland, Ukraine, Greece), Asia (Iran, Iraq, Vietnam), Africa (Congo, Sudan, Nigeria), South America (Argentina, Peru, Bolivia), and Oceania (Australia, New Zealand, Papua New Guinea) report their economic standing directly to the world.

Countries (darker shade) that report CPI through the IMF

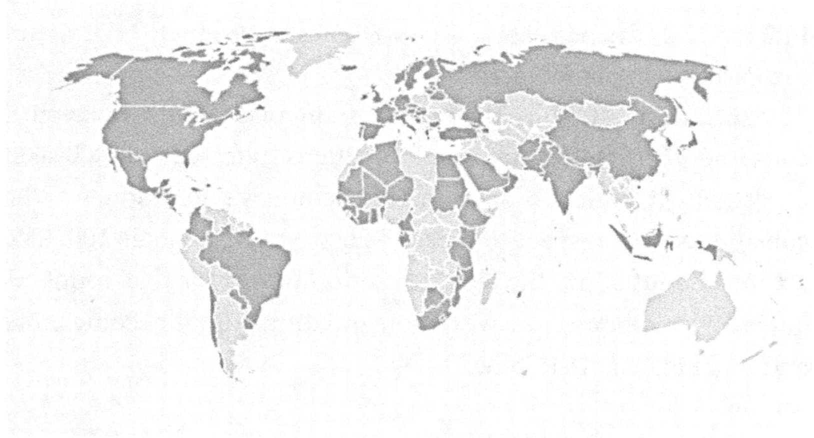

From the following graphs (adapted from Trading Economics) that track CPI from the countries representing the five political philosophies, it is clear that both extremes of the political spectrum (communist and free market countries) achieve low inflation indexes for their populations, whereas liberal countries experience higher inflation. These inflation indexes are achieved by very distinct means. Communist countries, and to an extent socialist countries, achieve it by subsidizing key goods in the basket of goods that are used to calculate CPI, thereby keeping them artificially lower than they really are. Free Market countries use the laws of offer and demand to maintain prices in the basket of goods low. They achieve this by keeping a number of similar goods well stocked, which result in prices kept on check while providing society with a wide variety of products.

China and Vietnam's inflation was caused by expansionary monetary policies and rising wages. As the cost of products increase due to higher wages, the companies are forced to raise prices in order to cover the costs. Inflation was controlled by subsidizing key goods in the basket of goods used to calculate CPI. Cuba did not report.

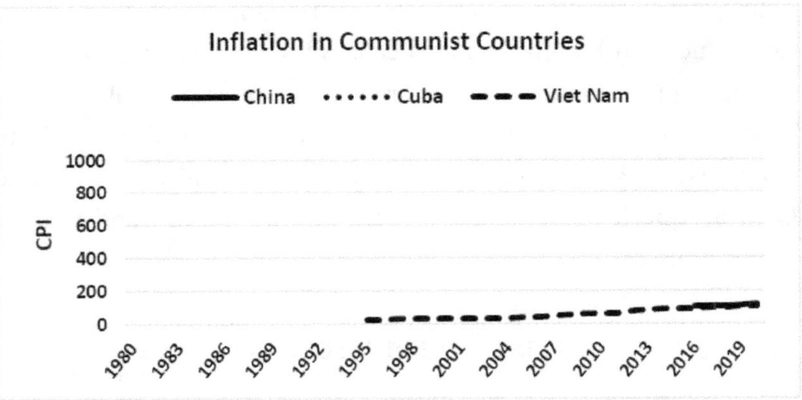

The cause of inflation in Singapore was the overheating of the economy and the open-door immigration policy that added nearly one million people to the existing 3.7 million. In Hong Kong, the rise of imported raw materials costs (caused by inflation in countries that are heavily dependent on exports of these commodities) or the fall in the value of the money in the foreign exchange markets, both of which increases the price of imported inputs, affected the CPI.

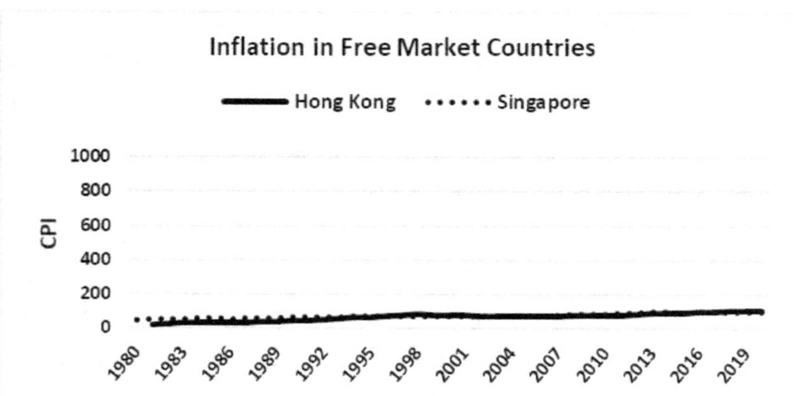

Algeria's longstanding need to diversify its economy away from hydrocarbons has gained fresh urgency since oil prices started falling dramatically in 2014. The ever-changing costs of living experienced in Bangladesh also causes the changes in poverty. In India, high demand and low production or supply of multiple commodities create a demand-supply gap, which leads to a hike in prices. Nicaragua's inflation is tied to the demand in the US and Central American markets for key agricultural exports and changes in remittances.

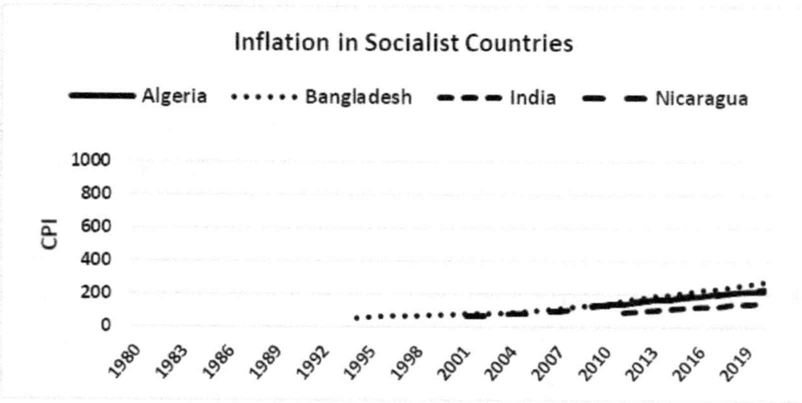

In Australia, the introduction of wage indexation (wage increases in line with increases in the CPI) kept inflation in check. In Canada, tax increases and the surge in economic growth lead to higher inflation as rising demand boosts wages and prices. In Sweden, weak international economic activity combined with low commodity prices, particularly for energy, have kept a lid on cost increases. In New Zealand, rapid population growth, shortages in housing supply, internal migration, immigration, cheap money, and foreign investors caused inflation.

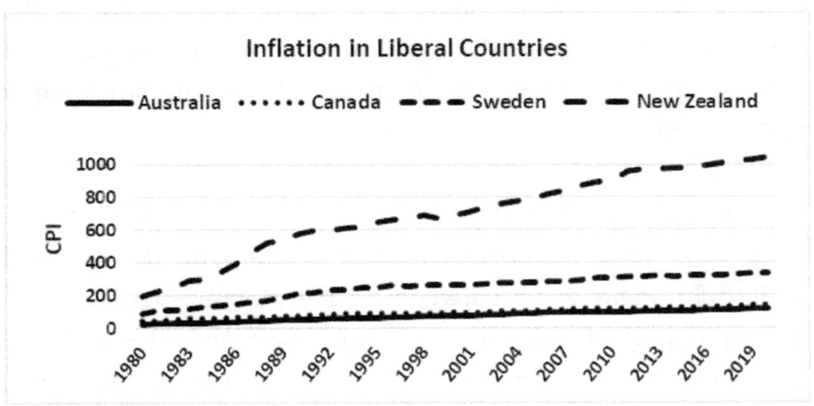

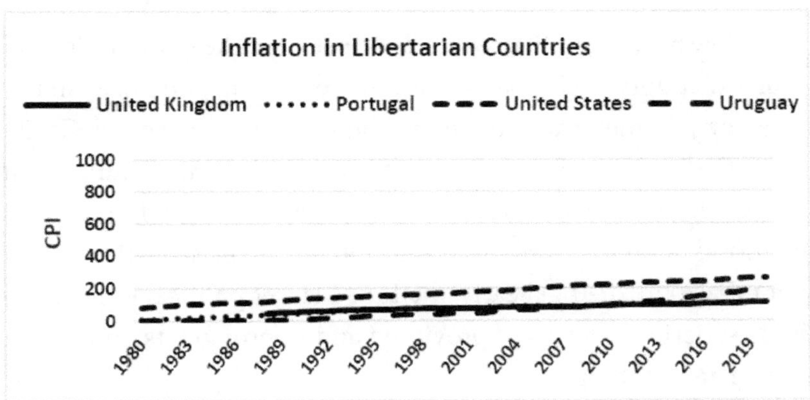

The UK targets an inflation rate of CPI = 2 ±1% while taking into account economic growth. The changes in the prices of transports (in particular fuels and lubricants) and food products principally affected the CPI in Portugal. In the US, the reduction of energy costs and the reduction of import costs has maintained inflation low. Uruguay's inflation is mainly caused by the impact of a drought and its peso depreciation.

Wealth – Gross Domestic Product (GDP) is the final value of the goods and services produced by a country. The greater the per capita GDP indicates that the country is producing and selling more goods, which means that there are jobs and an indication of better salaries.

From the graphs (adapted from Trading Economics), which track GDP from the countries representing the five political philosophies being analyzed, we observe very interesting differences that point to which political system works best for the people living in these countries. All the countries show a gradual growth in time, which translates into more money in people's pockets.

However, huge differences exist between the communist and socialist countries compared with the rest of the political systems. The key parameter to look at are the numbers on the Per Capita GDP (left) axis. We can see that for the communist countries, it ranges between nearly zero to $9,000, whereas for free market countries, it ranges from $10,000 to $60,000 in the same time frame (from 1980 to 2020). Clearly, the Free Market political philosophy is far superior in terms of providing and improving its population with material things.

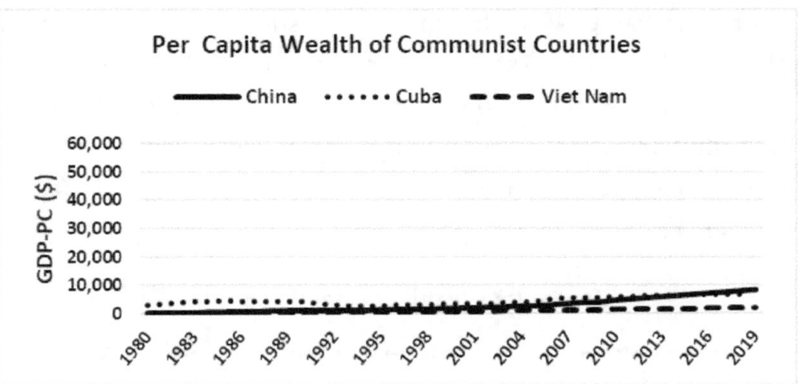

China's large-scale capital investment (financed by large domestic savings and foreign investment) produced rapid productivity growth. Cuba overestimates the value of its peso by artificially making it equal to the US dollar, indicating a manipulation of economic indexes. Vietnam's high domestic demand, strong manufacturing, processing industry, and high foreign investments produced economic growth.

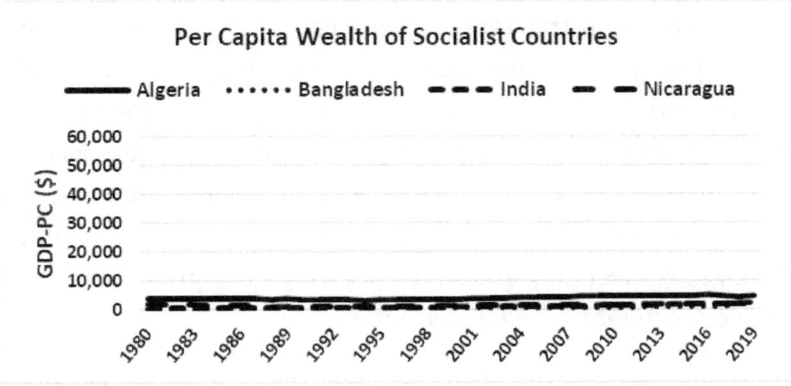

Algeria has one of the major economies in Africa, based largely on energy exports, but when prices drop or stay stagnant, its economy feels the effects. A decline in population growth and economic diversification is improving Bangladesh's economy.

Most of India's GDP is driven by domestic private consumption (the world's sixth-largest consumer market) as well as government spending, investment, and exports. Nicaragua's consistent political instability and conflict, high inequality between urban and rural populations, dependency on agricultural exports, and natural disasters keep the country poor.

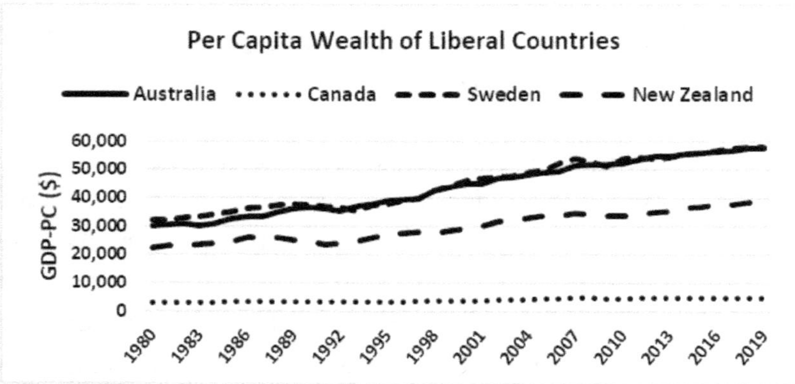

Mining, agriculture, government spending, and exports have contributed to Australia's high level of economic growth. Economic diversity in oil, manufacturing, and tourism are the key to Canada's wealth. Sweden is a competitive and highly liberalized open market economy under high-tech Capitalism. Farming, especially dairying, is significant, but other sectors such as forestry (and the production of paper and other wood products), horticulture, fishing, deer farming, and manufacturing have produced a more balanced economy in New Zealand.

The sectors that contribute most to the U.K.'s wealth are services, manufacturing, construction, and tourism. Portugal's economy is dominated by services and manufacturing, which constitute a significant share of wealth, while agricultural output is still relatively minor but growing. The US is wealthy because of its abundant natural resources, well-developed infrastructure, high productivity mixed with a culture of entrepreneurship, a financial system that supports it, abundant energy, immigration, smaller and more decentralized government, and top research universities. Meat, soya beans, and wood are the main exports for Uruguay, and its well-educated workforce provides for a promising future in manufacturing and high-tech industries.

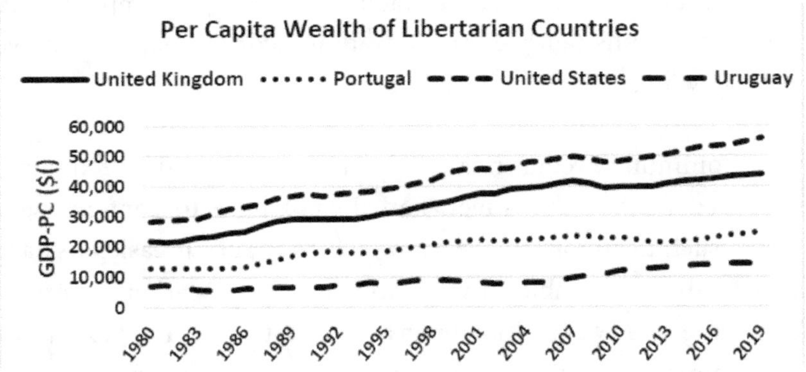

Hong Kong's effective financial services, tourism, trading and logistics, and professional and producer services are due to its low tax policy. Singapore's domestic development is driven by exports in electronics manufacturing and machinery, financial services, tourism, and the world's busiest cargo seaport.

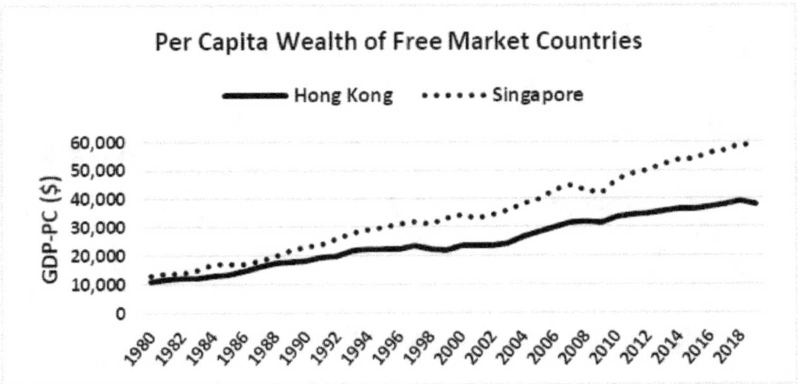

Unemployment - Percent unemployment is the percent of the labor force that is jobless in the country. The smallest unemployment rates mean that more people have a job and, therefore, a better life. Again, both political extremes appear to present the best options in terms of securing jobs for their population. The Communist and Free Trade systems maintain an unemployment rate below 5%. The other political systems are much more variable, which indicate they are somewhat unstable with respect to employment. From the graphs (adapted from Trading Economics), we observe the following:

Communist countries completely control the economic activities, control the wages, and do not have to contend with issues such as unions and welfare, which makes it easier to have everybody who is able to work working. Free Market countries' economies are by definition open and unrestricted. The labor force is dynamic and subject to the laws of market offer and demand. Since the government's foremost role is to create the most favorable conditions to attract jobs, unemployment is kept low.

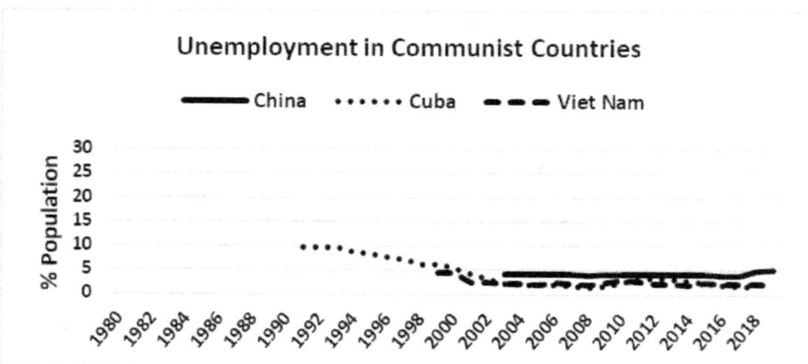

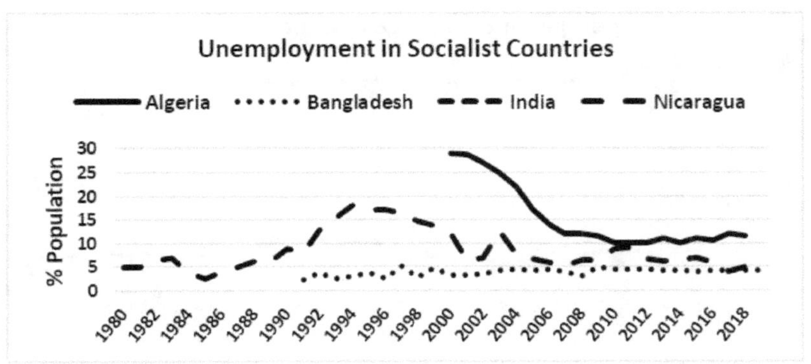

Unemployment in Socialist Countries
Algeria
Bangladesh
India
Nicaragua
% Population
30
25
20
15
10
5
0
1980
1982
1984
1986
1988
1990
1992
1994
1996
1998
2000
2002
2004
2006
2008
2010
2012
2014
2016
2018

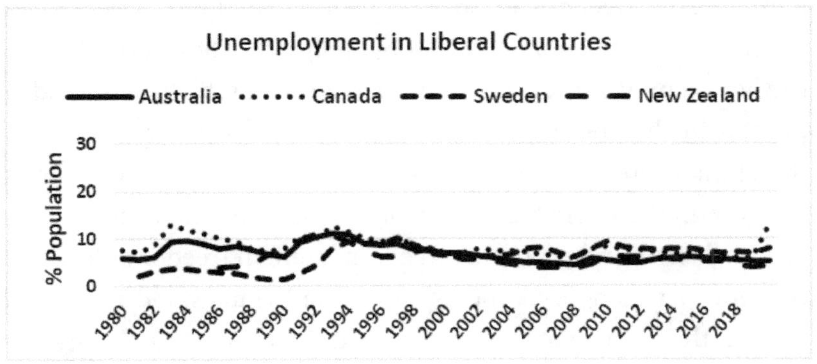

Unemployment in Liberal Countries
Australia
Canada
Sweden
New Zealand
% Population
30
20
10
0
1980
1982
1984
1986
1988
1990
1992
1994
1996
1998
2000
2002
2004
2006
2008
2010
2012
2014
2016
2018

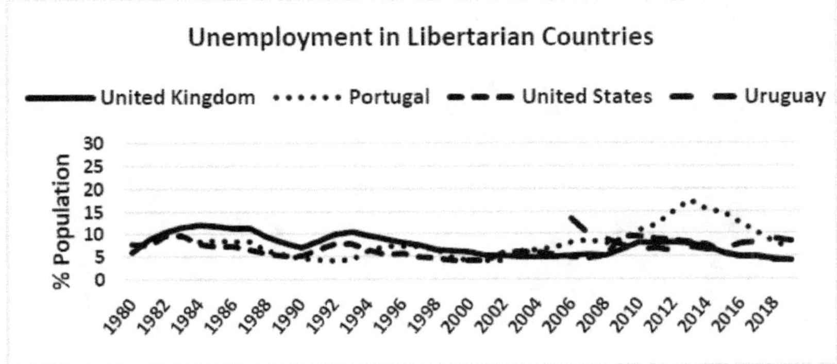

Unemployment in Libertarian Countries
United Kingdom
Portugal
United States
Uruguay
% Population
30
25
20
15
10
5
0
1980
1982
1984
1986
1988
1990
1992
1994
1996
1998
2000
2002
2004
2006
2008
2010
2012
2014
2016
2018

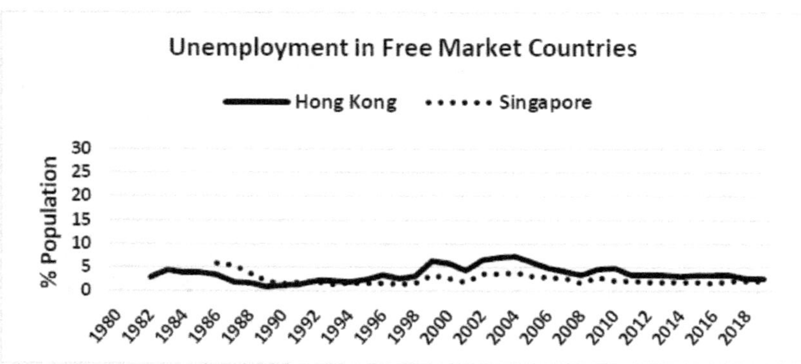

Freedom - Citizen's liberties, on the other hand, can be measured by freedom of speech, freedom of press, freedom of assembly, and freedom to exercise religion. These liberties are further secured if they are accompanied by a set of rules for due process in the law. The Cato Institute introduces the concept of the Human Freedom Index, which "presents the state of human freedom in the world based on a broad measure that encompasses personal, civil, and economic freedom. Human freedom is a social concept that recognizes the dignity of individuals and is defined here as the absence of coercive constraints". After analyzing the indicators for each country, they created a map that shows how free each country really is.

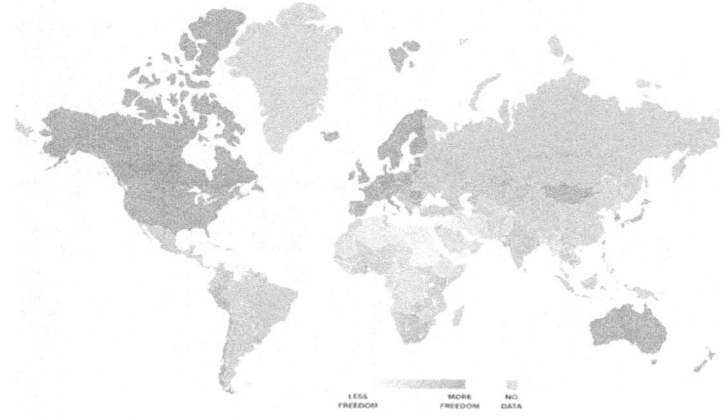

The Human Freedom Index presents a broad measure of human freedom and uses 76 distinct indicators of personal and economic freedom in the following areas:

Rule of Law, Security and Safety, Movement, Religion, Association, Assembly, and Civil Society, Expression and Information, Identity and Relationships, Size of Government, Legal System and Property Rights, Access to Sound Money, Freedom to Trade Internationally, Regulation of Credit, Labor, and Business.

Tabulating the Personal Freedom and Economic Freedom for each of the countries representing the five different political philosophies we are tracking, we get the following graph:

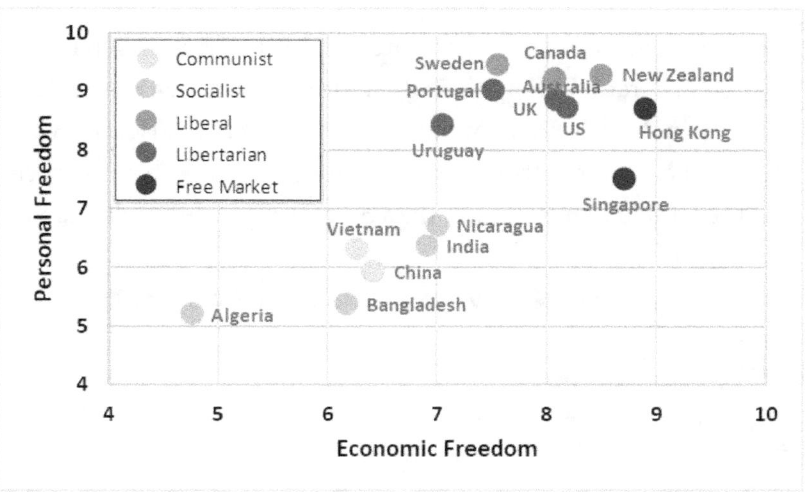

It is clear that there is a wide gap between communist (China and Vietnam – Cuba did not report) and socialist countries (Algeria, Bangladesh, India, Nicaragua) compared to the rest of the political philosophies in terms of freedom. There is no surprise that liberal countries (Australia, Canada, New Zealand, Sweden) give precedence to personal freedom compared to economic freedom, whereas the Free Market countries (Hong Kong, Singapore) prioritize the opposite. The libertarian countries (Portugal, United States, United Kingdom, Uruguay) probably provide a good balance between these liberties.

Immigration - Immigration is a measure of how attractive a country is compared with other countries. The more a country is seen as a destination to immigrate, implies that the country is probably wealthy, and its system of government is effective at providing more opportunities to succeed in life than obviously the country of origin, but also more opportunities to succeed than other countries in the world.

The Migration Policy Institute provides migration data to the 100,000 accuracy. Taking their data for the countries representing the five political philosophies, we can clearly discern which countries are more attractive for migrants. It is with no surprise that the United States is more than 5 times more desirable than the

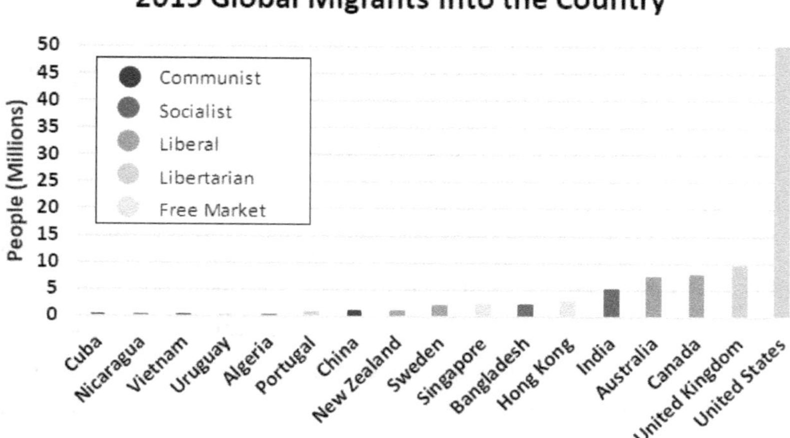

2019 Global Migrants Into the Country

next best, which happens to be the United Kingdom, among the countries we are tracking. Another curious fact is that Hong Kong, a small (427 square miles) Special Administrative Region of the People's Republic of China (with 3.7 million square miles), attracts nearly three times the immigrants than mainland China.

　　　　　　　　　　　　　　　　　　　

Analysis of the Findings

This generalized socio-economic analysis is sufficient to draw clear conclusions about which political philosophy is more effective at creating what people crave the most: jobs, opportunities to develop goals or dreams, freedom of expression, freedom to worship, fair laws that apply to everyone equally, and a government that guarantees all those things for generations to come.

Communist and its "light" version in socialist countries are ruled by dictators. They only believe in democracy as a means to obtain power. Once in power, they are not willing to relinquish it in fair elections. They will intervene and disrupt the voting system to make sure they will remain in power. They will work to transform the government mechanisms, eliminating any existing balance of power, eliminating dissenting expressions, and eventually replacing God with the State.

Liberal countries and, to a lesser extent, libertarian countries, have increasingly been lured by the socialist opium. They are being tempted to stay in power not so much by the typical socialist ideology but by another more recent political philosophy: Globalism. Globalists believe the problems of humanity can be resolved with "democratic globalism." Democratic globalism is the idea that all people matter, no matter where they live, and that universal freedom and human rights can be fostered for all mankind in what they call "world citizens." That is, they believe in civic globalism and that by thinking globally and acting locally, they can affect positive change across all barriers. Countries, their borders, and their laws should not exist anymore.

Of course, "democratic globalism" is a farce. It is just a "feel-good" concept that is impossible to achieve by "normal" democratic means. It goes against the natural human tendency to belong to a familiar group. The USSR fragmented back to the original republics once the communists lost their grip on them in 1991 for a reason. That same reason pushes the Catalans to want to separate from Spain and so on. Globalization is a pretext to gain power without providing a realistic government plan to solve the problems at hand. Logic indicates that if a system cannot solve the problems of a small territory (a country), it will definitely not solve the problems of the globe.

The left has discovered that they make political strides with a "crisis" agenda. In the past, they used evident issues, such as fair labor force treatment, environmental pollution, or the dependence on foreign oil, as political platforms to advance their big government agenda. These issues have largely been solved by ingenuity and technology. The left then figured that virtually impossible issues had to be used as crises in order to perpetuate themselves in power. Items such as racism, social injustice, sexuality, or climate change are the new crises. They pretend that by transferring the issues to the global realm and trying to show how unsurmountable the problems are, voters would support them.

The left does not talk about (and the mainstream press does not report) that it is actually their policies that perpetuate racism in the most awful way. Hillary Clinton said in an interview: "I admire Margaret Sanger enormously, her courage, her tenacity, her vision…" Sanger created what eventually became the Planned Parenthood Federation of America, the same group that targets abortions in black neighborhoods. This is what Sanger says about her "Negro Project," speaking to a Ku Klux Klan group: "The gradual suppression, elimination and eventual extinction of defective stocks, those human weeds which threaten the blooming of the finest flowers of American civilization." This begs the question: which side is actually racist? The one that wants to provide the same opportunity to thrive in society to everyone or the one that constantly reminds us of the racial differences among us?

Global warming, which now has been renamed "climate change," blames the current increase in temperature of earth's atmosphere to the increase in carbon dioxide due to human activity. The problem with that narrative is that earth's average atmospheric temperature is very variable and does not follow the trend suggested by climate change advocates, as shown in the figure.

The figure shows that earth's average atmospheric temperature has varied from plus 0.44°C in 1428 to minus 0.28°C in 1680, as compared to the year 1770 temperature. These temperature peaks hardly correspond to the Industrial Revolution period (1760-1840), when the heavy atmospheric emissions began. Recent temperature variations are well within the natural range experienced in our past when there were no internal combustion engines. The famous "hockey stick" shape graph used by environmental activists pushing the global warming narrative "is primarily an artefact of poor data handling, obsolete data and incorrect calculation of principal components" according to the authors of the scientific paper that published the graph. In other words, the temperature

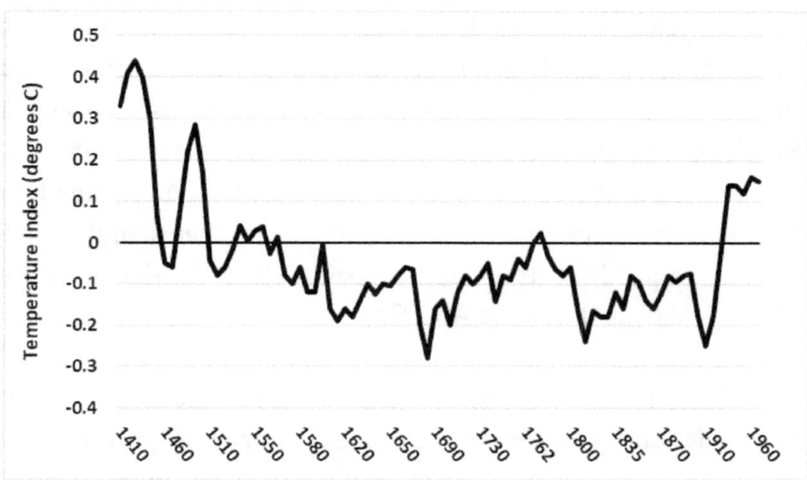

Northern Hemisphere Temperature Variations Showing Temperature Swings are Normal (Adapted from McIntyre & McKitrick, 2003)

data was actually fudged to fit the global warming narrative. The atmospheric temperature variations logically points to our planet's main source of energy: the sun and its cyclic solar activity.

Facts are the biggest enemy for socialists and globalists; that is why they especially target youngsters who have been preconditioned by teachers and professors to blindly believe in this stuff. If the democratic option does not gain them power, they adopt the "revolutionary" option, which is to cause confusion, unrest, rioting, and destruction until they do get into power.

In the meantime, globalists have the support of the largest transnational companies that have setup their industrial facilities in developing countries where they have established connections with corrupt leaders and governments, pay low wages, do not need to contend with labor laws, and pollute the environment with little or no control. For example, GE Appliances is an iconic American home appliance manufacturer founded in 1905. Since 2016, the Louisville, Kentucky-based company is majority-owned by Chinese multinational home appliances company Haier. GM Company is another iconic American corporation founded in 1908 and headquartered in Detroit, Michigan, that manufactures vehicles. Since 2011, the company sold 50% of its shares to the Chinese SAIC and now is SAIC-GM.

The rich and the very rich investors in these transnational companies obviously do not want to jeopardize their investments. As a result, they heavily finance the campaigns of candidates who will support the globalist agenda. Some of the very rich finance globalists because they simply are evil. They made their money using the Free Market system but now want to exert political power by replacing it with Globalism.

A growing number of people have figured this out and are now opposing this pernicious agenda. Even though billions of dollars have been spent in support of globalist positions and candidates in the last 30 years, Brexit in 2016 prevailed, and Donald Trump won the US presidential election in 2017. We will see if these movements will prevail.

Conclusion

Communism and Socialism have been tried by many countries during the past century. Not one country that has adopted it has improved the lives of its citizens. The only people who gain from the government control of its citizenry are the self-imposed rulers. They and their families become rich while the countries become devastated, and those citizens that complain are jailed or assassinated. Communism and Socialism in the last century have left a trail of more *civilian* deaths than all the wars put together. An estimated 110 million have been killed by systemic starvation, executions, labor camps, and ethnic cleansing. This figure does not include deaths that occurred during wars.

We are not perfect. Thus no political system is perfect. Since something created can never be better than its creator, political systems are in many respects flawed. This is especially true when talking about politics, which brings the worst of humanity because not many leaders can handle power and ambition. In spite of this, only Capitalism through a government with clear and balanced separation of powers has ever lifted people and countries out of poverty. Like everything, there are good capitalist systems, and there are better ones.

Unfortunately, no pure free market economies actually exist in the world. All markets have in some ways been constrained by politicians for their own gain. However, economists who measure the degree of freedom in markets have found a generally positive relationship between Free Markets and economic well-being.

Case in Point - There are many cases of countries that demonstrate the benefits of Capitalism. A good example is my homeland country of Peru, which I am very familiar with. Since very early in its history as a republic, Peru could be defined as being a democracy under a system of oligarchy/aristocracy. This until 1968, when a military coup occurred. The democratically elected president was removed by force and sent to exile. This was not the first coup during its history that changed governance in Peru. However, this was the first communist military coup ever in its history. Expropiated companies were consolidated into government run entities, starting with the American International Petroleum Company.

Soon after, everyone who owned farmland was targeted with the moto: "The land is for those who work it." The government then confiscated every hacienda. Not before long, journeymen with no education or skills were told by the government that they were part owners of the agro-industrial facility they used to work for. As "owners," workers did not feel the need to "get their hands dirty anymore" and began to slack off. Production soon plummeted. Once an exporter of sugar, rice, etc., Peru began to import these goods. One year the government even had to import potatoes. Imagine! The land from which the potato was originally cultivated even by the pre-Inca peoples now had to import it from China, of all places! A disaster.

The country endured this for 12 long years. Of course, there was no longer freedom of the press, and during this time, even the Church (and the citizens) were extremely careful about criticizing the military. It could easily land them in jail. The only way to get a fair shake with the legal system was to have some connection with the military. The military had absolute power. They were living the good life while the people endured curfews, food shortages, restrictions on car usage, travel restrictions, etc.

When the military left power in 1980, the president who was ousted in 1968 was elected again. The country that he inherited was completely destroyed. It was heavily indebted, and production output was at its lowest as mining, agriculture, and manufacturing centers were still in the hands of communist cooperatives and the like. On top of this, the power displaced communists were not happy and wanted to take back power by all means possible.

In the political arena, the communist party began to take force. In society, the communists began to first enlist students and later forced highland farmers from little towns to enroll in what they called "the Shining Path," and begin the destruction of governmental institutions through terrorist attacks. If the farmers refused, they were lined up at the town square or outside of town, and they were shot to death. The terrorists partnered with the cocaine drug lords to obtain armament in exchange for protection and raided many mining facilities and police stations to acquire more armament and explosives. They used the explosives to blow up power towers to cause city blackouts and used the armaments to attack governmental headquarters. Anfo (a mix of fuel and fertilizer) car bombs exploded daily, in different city locations, killing and injuring many people. Car bomb explosions throughout the city were our morning alarm clock indicating the end of the curfew time. Lima, the "City of Gardens," began to look like a city at war. Concrete barricades closed certain streets, sandbag walls were erected at key locations, people began to reinforce windows and doors with iron bars and electrified wires on top of walls.

As the 1990 elections approached, it was almost certain that the communist would take power, this time by democratic means. There was no clear political candidate to represent the center or right factions of the country. Unexpectedly an unknown candidate began campaigning and, to the surprise of many, was elected president. Two years later the new president dissolved Congress, which impeded him to promulgate necessary legislation to get the country on track toward an "orthodox economic standing." He conducted an internal coup that completely transformed the political system, stopping internal political and judicial strife that obstructed the detention, judgment, and incarceration of terrorists. He sold all the communist governmental companies to the private sector and in 1993 was able to capture the heads of the two main terrorist groups, along with most of the fighters, summarily judge them in military courts, and incarcerate them. On 28 August 2003, the Peruvian Truth and Reconciliation Commission reported that an estimated 69,280 persons were killed by terrorism in Peru from 1980 to 2000.

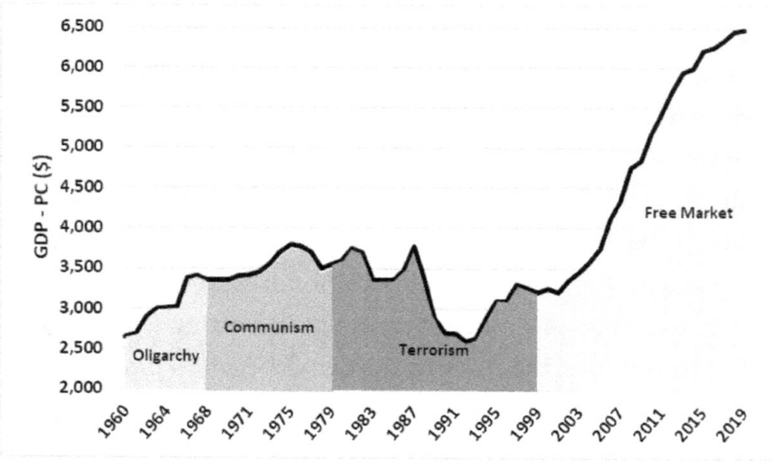

Change of Per Capita Wealth in Peru (1960-2019)

Looking at the Trading Economics graph of the the per capita country wealth for Peru over the last 59 years, we can see how Communism did little to improve the GDP, which remained stagnated until 1987, when the economy took a dip as terrorism ravaged the country. Then we observe some improvement when terrorism was quenched, and the economy was again opened to a freer market, still shackled by dictatorship. Wealth began to skyrocket starting 2002 as never before when democracy was established under a rather libertarian political scheme. Poverty in Peru went from 60% in 2000 to 20% in 2018. This example cannot explain it clearer; Communism is counterproductive, and Capitalism works! Nevertheless, government corruption during this growth period by, ironically, center-left and left peruvian presidents, have robbed its citizens of a fair distribution of wealth.

Why is the US Exceptional?

The US is a unique country in the world for many reasons. It is the only country that has a philosophy behind its Constitution (a list of principles) whereas other countries have prescriptive constitutions (a list of rules).

The US Constitution, signed September 17, 1787, pulls the essence of the creation of the country based on inalienable or absolute principles. The founders recognized that these principles come not from the State (like is believed by the other countries) but from our Creator. The basis for the Constitution and the Bill of Rights goes beyond the Ten Commandments given to Moses by God. They are a sort of translation of the law in terms of socio-political tenets in order to obtain a fair system of government.

The Constitution and the Bill of Rights set the policy for the country, or its reason to exist. The details are filled in by the Amendments, which act as support posts that hold the platform containing the policy. Amendments can only be added, never removed. Otherwise, the central principles would certainly crumble. Ask yourself, who is currently attempting to undermine the First and Second Amendment? Why are they trying to destroy the central principles of this country?

Commentary

Besides the economic indicators, all of which the US leads among the entirety of the libertarian countries, the US mostly leads in immigration. Most people around the world prefer to come to the US as supposed to other countries. Any country in that enviable position would be very selective of who to accept as a resident. Instead, politicians chose to put on blinders and succumb to special interest groups rather than think on the well-being of the country. As long as farms, industries, and commercial facilities have enough cheap labor, they pay little attention to the porous border. However, a growing number of citizens began to complain that public services were being overwhelmed. Public schools, for example, began to increase the student/teacher ratio, affecting the progress of their students and reducing the quality of education. This situation triggered an increase in the education budgets. However, spending more money not necessarily improves the quality of education, as most of the additional funds went to administrative and useless education programs. The following map shows how much each state spends annually per student in public education versus the US education ranking for the border states. It illustrates the impact undocumented children have on the education system.

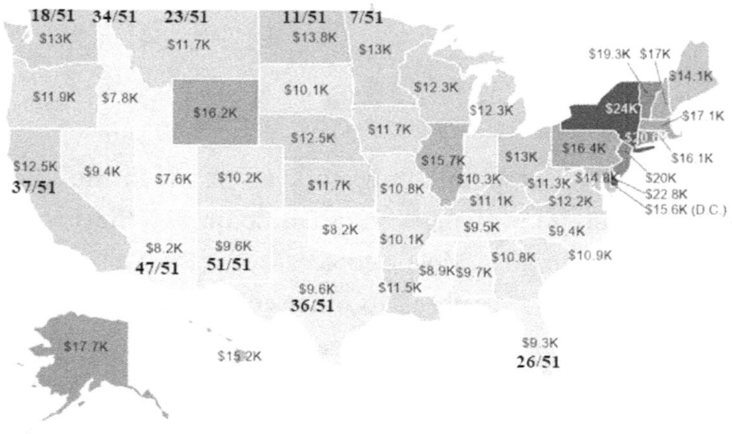

2018 Public School Spending per Student and US Ranking of State School Systems in Border States (Including Washington, DC)

According to the Federation for American Immigration Reform, back in 2010, the cost of undocumented immigrants to the country was $28.8 billion, and the collection from their taxes was $9.5 billion, which gave a deficit of $19.3 billion that year. Nine years later (2019), the same organization determined that the deficit was $115.9 billion for that year! Something had to be done. Estimates on the number of undocumented immigrants living in the US range from 10.5 million to 12 million. Many think this is an underestimation and undocumented immigrants in the US are most probably about 20 million and rapidly growing.

Besides the undocumented immigrants, there are about 3 million legal immigrants entering the US each year. They come from all over the world. We assume they come to get a chance at making true for themselves the "American Dream." You would think they want to work hard, improve the lives for themselves and their families, and enjoy life in freedom while pursuing happiness.

However, a growing number of these *legal* immigrants develop a grudge. Some are mistreated for their looks or their accents. This happens everywhere in the globe to newcomer migrants. My grandparents endured it when they came to the US from Russia, my parents endured it when they, in turn, migrated to South America, and we endured it when we migrated back to the US. It certainly happened to immigrants who arrived in the country in previous centuries as well. Italians, Irish, Poles, Russians, and Germans were discriminated against when they first arrived. Later were Jews, Puerto Ricans, Mexicans, etc. They did not complain or whine about their predicament. They moved on and "plowed ahead." They strived to integrate, which they eventually did.

What is unconceivable is the legal immigrant who wants to change the American system and desires to implement in the US the failed policies used by their countries of origin. Why come to the "land of the free" if they would rather live under a different political philosophy? Did they not come to the US because the system was awful where they came from? Are they really here to pursue the American Dream or to take advantage of the system and ruin it for the rest of us?

Actually, what they are going to accomplish, if they succeed, is to ruin it for the new generation that will come after. Their own children and grandchildren. This befuddles me. You sacrifice everything to come to the US but ruin it for your offspring. It does not make any sense.

Talking About Religion

To talk about God is a bit complicated because you have to first remove from the path a big stumbling block. That stumbling block is religion. Religion is having faith in a humanly created faith system. There is no way you can discuss religion without hurting "human feelings" because "feelings" cannot be discussed. You cannot argue for or against how someone feels about something. You can only discuss facts, ideas, and concepts.

Religion is a means created by humans to reach out to God. Religions supposedly provide a recipe to please God. But there are *many* religions. However, logic determines there is only *one* God. The logical first question would be, which is "the *true* religion?" Common sense indicates that there is a flaw in trying to answer that question. Why? Well, as mentioned before, if religion is man-made, discussing religion would be like discussing feelings. Each person has an opinion based on a mix of feelings, ideas, and traditions. There is no truth to be discussed because each person has their own version of the truth.

With this, I do not pretend to insinuate that people cannot discuss their versions of truth. But this discussion would have to be very diplomatic, with the understanding that the matter being discussed is a simple exchange of ideas with no expected outcome other than the proverbial "we agree to disagree." Most people do not like that kind of discussion because it is frustrating and leads nowhere.

Most people like discussions that arrive at conclusions. Most have ideas which they try to demonstrate by proving and convincing others that their concepts are correct. This gives the advantage to those who express themselves very well verbally, not necessarily those who have the best ideas. Those who do not have them or cannot express themselves well verbally usually stay on the sidelines left out of the discussion except for occasional interjections here and there that typically are ignored. This is why I write this book.

If we cannot discuss religion, then what? Well, then we need to consider an analysis of the writings about God instead of trying to decipher God through religion. This is quite involved. Maybe that is why no one wants to discuss it. In order to move on, there are two paradigms or concepts that need to be resolved and absolved in your mind.

The first paradigm is this:

If you believe there is only *one* God, you must believe there is only *one* truth.

If you believe there is one God, then that God has to be explained *one* way. In other words, there is only one truth about God. What is truth, you may ask? Well, truth is the manifestation of reality from the exclusive perspective of God. Not my perspective, not yours, not anyone's. Only God's.

The second paradigm is this:

If there is *one* truth, there must be only *one* Word of God.

If God exists, He had to manifest Himself to us, His creation. God had to manifest Himself by providing a record of His truth. In other words, God had to provide us His manifesto of reality, what some call "the Word of God" or His story. Otherwise, how would He make Himself known? If God created us, He would have to have made Himself known to us. God makes Himself apparent to us in two ways; His story and the longing we all have in our hearts to worship Him. His story is His word. The longing is that emptiness we all feel when we do not obey Him. So strong is that longing that those people who say they do not believe in God replace it with believing in some aspect of God's creation. Believing in something superior to us is innate and necessary to humans.

We cannot move forward with the discussion about God unless you have cleared these two paradigms. To some people, these are just given; it is just logical. But to some, these are stumbling blocks. If they are stumbling blocks to you, take your time, read the paradigms again and ponder about them until they make sense to you.

So, it is clear we have moved from talking about religion to talking about *the* Word of God. They are definitely not the same thing. This is important to have clear in your mind.

What qualifies as *the* Word of God? Well, *the* word or story must cover important portions of human spiritual history and provide explanation for important facts such as: How did everything get created? Why do we sin? Since sin separates us from God, what are we expected to do to get back into good graces with God?

The explanatory story must be logical because God is logical. It will include supernatural events because God is, by definition, supernatural. But the story must be credible. The story must also be simple enough that anyone can read it and understand the message. God is everyone's God. He does not make any distinctions between gender, mental abilities, social, or economical standings. He wants *all* His human creation to know *the* truth. His truth.

What follows is the *logic* behind the search or the quest for *the* Word of God:

If God is perfect, He only accepts perfection onto itself. If humankind is sinful, it is imperfect and unfit to stand before God.

Since it is impossible for an imperfect being to save itself, humankind requires a savior to be accepted by God. Sin is innate to humans. No one learns to be sinful. Kids lie, are egotistical, aggressive against other kids, etc., from an early age. Nobody had to teach them these things. Parents struggle (or they should) until their kids become adults to teach them to behave correctly. Religions offer a recipe to try to overcome sin, but they only offer a placebo. Proof of this is that religious people are no better than non-religious people in terms of committing sins.

God created us perfectly, but Original Sin separates us from God. God created us with a freewill in order to prove that we love Him. Otherwise, we would be like robots doing what we are programmed to do. And that is not what God wants. He wants people who are able to discern between good and evil, even in our current sinful state, and struggle to please Him. If good would be easy to do and obtain, it would have no value. Things that require work give us the most satisfaction and value. Now, "being good" or "doing more good than evil" is not good enough for God, but we will touch on that later on.

God is omniscient (all-knowing) and knew we would sin, but still God loves us.
If God loves us, He would give us a way out of our predicament.

What story or Word of God tells us how to get back in communion and into good graces with Him?

We have already concluded that there should be only *one* true story. If that is true, why are there so many religions?

Religions are a result of people needing to belong to a like-minded group. Religions are man's attempt to reach God. Religions have evolved; they have changed based on adjustments in traditions and changes in human culture and mentality over time. However, *the* true story, by definition, must remain one solid, unchanged, unwavering story: *the* Word of God.

Does your religion describe a way to being saved? Are you sure your religion coincides with *the* story regarding being saved? Are you willing to risk your eternal life by not checking for yourself what His story actually says?

How can you verify if His story (the Word of God) is real?

Well, as was mentioned, it must be ancient but must be credible (the actors must not be mythological beings). Of course, the story will be filled with supernatural events because God is supernatural. This is the first act of faith from our part. Believing in God is difficult to some. If the evidence in the complexity in design of the microcosm (what we can observe through a microscope), the macrocosm (what we can observe in plain sight), and of the astronomic (what we observe through a telescope) is not enough to convince you of the existence of God, then there is truly little I can say here to convince you. This is something you need to contemplate and ponder on your own.

Take a basic biology book and consider the wonderful design of a cell. All its parts have specific functions. And at a given time, all these parts orchestrate in perfect harmony to subdivide and in seconds create another identical cell. Then consider the group of cells that form an organ. Take the eye, for example. There are so many specialized cells working in unison to form an eye that is mind-boggling! Consider the eyes of the trilobites, extinct marine arachnomorph arthropods (a large marine rollie pollie) supposedly from the Cambrian Period (allegedly 520 million years ago), which disappeared during a "major extinction event" at the end of the Permian Period (supposedly 250 million years ago). They had compound eyes similar to the eyes of today's insects and crustaceans. How can an organism allegedly in Earth's early stages of animal evolution have such complex eyes?

Take an astronomy book. Look at the thousands of constellations that exist in just a small portion of the universal expanse. Each constellation, a universe in magnitude in itself, is composed of millions of suns in tidy spirals. Each sun with a set of planets orderly circling it. All planets barren, too hot, too cold, or too toxic to support life except one: Earth, which is situated in a secondary branch of one of the main spiral arms that form the Milky Way. It is a fact that the universe is expanding at a rate of 160,000 mph, then how can these constellations still present themselves as perfectly ordered spirals if they supposedly are 13.8 billion years old?

What are the possible writings of God?

___

Of the thousands of religions, only four writings *claim* to be from God. These are The Book of Mormon, The Koran, The Vedas, and The Bible. The following summaries have been taken from Wikipedia (2021) excerpts in order to minimize personal bias. Read them and then ask yourself; which one is more credible? Which one makes more sense? Which one would I deposit my faith in?

The Book of Mormon
Founder: Joseph Smith
Location: Wayne County, New York
Date: 1823
Converts: 16.6 million
Belief System:

- Claim that "total" apostasy overcame the church following apostolic times and that the Mormon Church (founded in 1830) is the "restored church."
- Claim that God the Father was once a man and that he then progressed to godhood (exalted, immortal man with a flesh-and-bone body).
- Believe that the Trinity consists not of three persons in one God but rather of three distinct gods. According to Mormonism, there are potentially many thousands of gods besides these three.
- Believe that humans, like God the Father, can go through a process of exaltation to godhood.

- Believe that Jesus Christ was the firstborn spirit-child of the heavenly Father and a heavenly Mother. Jesus then progressed to deity in the spirit world. Jesus was later physically conceived in Mary's womb as the literal "only begotten" Son of God the Father in the flesh (though many present-day Mormons remain somewhat vague as to how this occurred).

Summary:

According to Joseph Smith, he was seventeen years of age when an angel of God named Moroni appeared to him and said that a collection of ancient writings was buried in a nearby hill in present-day Wayne County, New York, engraved on golden plates by ancient prophets. The writings were said to describe a people whom God had led from Jerusalem to the Western hemisphere 600 years before Jesus' birth. According to the narrative, Moroni was the last prophet among these people and had buried the record, which God had promised to bring forth in the latter days. Smith stated that this vision occurred on the evening of September 21, 1823, and that on the following day, via divine guidance, he located the burial location of the plates on this hill; was instructed by Moroni to meet him at the same hill on September 22nd of the following year to receive further instructions; and that, in four years from this date, the time would arrive for "bringing them forth" (translating them). Smith's description of these events recounts that he was allowed to take the plates on September 22, 1827, exactly four years from that date, and was directed to translate them into English.

Smith's first published description of the plates said that the plates "had the appearance of gold." They were described by Martin Harris, one of Smith's early scribes, as "fastened together in the shape of a book by wires." Smith called the engraved writing on the plates "reformed Egyptian." A portion of the text on the plates was also "sealed" according to his account, so its content was not included in the contents of the Book of Mormon. In addition to Smith's account regarding the plates, eleven others stated that they saw the golden plates and, in some cases, handled them. Their written testimonies are known as the Testimony of Three Witnesses and the Testimony of Eight Witnesses. These statements have been published in most editions of the Book of Mormon.

In 1829, work resumed on the Book of Mormon, with the assistance of Oliver Cowdery, and was completed in a short period (April–June 1829). Smith said that he then returned the plates to Moroni upon the publication of the book. The Book of Mormon went on sale at the bookstore of E. B. Grandin in Palmyra, New York, on March 26, 1830.

Critique: Since its first publication and distribution, critics of the Book of Mormon have claimed that it was fabricated by Smith and that he drew material and ideas from various sources rather than translating an ancient record. Works that have been suggested as sources include the King James Bible, The Wonders of Nature, View of the Hebrews, and an unpublished manuscript written by Solomon Spalding.

Most of the archaeological, historical, and scientific communities do not consider the Book of Mormon an ancient record of actual historical events. Their skepticism tends to focus on four main areas:

1. The lack of correlation between locations described in the Book of Mormon and known, intact American archaeological sites.
2. References to animals, plants, metals, and technologies in the Book of Mormon that archaeological or scientific studies have found no evidence of in post-Pleistocene, pre-Columbian America, frequently referred to as anachronisms. Items typically listed include cattle, horses, asses, oxen, sheep, swine, goats, elephants, wheat, steel, brass, chains, iron, scimitars, and chariots.
3. The lack of widely accepted linguistic connections between any Native American languages and Near Eastern languages.
4. The lack of DNA evidence linking any Native American group to the ancient Near East.

Counter: Most adherents of the Latter Day Saint movement consider the Book of Mormon to generally be a historically accurate account. Within the Latter Day Saint movement, there are several apologetic groups that disagree with the skeptics and seek to reconcile the discrepancies in diverse ways. Among these apologetic groups, much work has been published by Foundation for Ancient Research and Mormon Studies (FARMS) and Foundation for Apologetic Information & Research (FAIR), defending the Book of Mormon as a literal history, countering arguments critical of its historical authenticity, or reconciling historical and scientific evidence with the text. One of the more common recent arguments is the limited geography model, which states that the people mentioned in the Book of Mormon covered only a limited geographical region in either Mesoamerica, South America, or the Great Lakes area. The Latter Day Saints Church has published material indicating that science will support the historical authenticity of the Book of Mormon.

The Koran
Founder: Muhammad
Location: Mecca, Saudi Arabia
Date: AD 632
Converts: 1.9 billion
Belief System:

- Muslims worship one, all-knowing God, who in Arabic is known as Allah, under whom they live in complete submission.
- Nothing can happen without Allah's permission, but humans have freewill.
- Believe several prophets were sent to teach Allah's law. They respect some of the same prophets as Jews and Christians, including Abraham, Moses, Noah, and Jesus. Muslims contend that Muhammad was the final prophet.
- The Koran (or Quran) is the major holy text of Islam. The Hadith is another important book. Muslims also revere some material found in the Judeo-Christian Bible.
- Believe there will be a day of judgment and life after death.
- A central idea in Islam is "jihad," which means "struggle." Muslims believe it refers to internal and external efforts to defend their faith.
- When Muhammad died, there was debate over who should replace him as leader. This led to a schism in Islam, and two major sects emerged: the Sunnis and the Shiites. Sunnis make up nearly 90 percent of Muslims

worldwide. They accept that the first four caliphs were the true successors to Muhammad. Shiite Muslims believe that only the caliph Ali and his descendants are the real successors to Muhammad.

Summary:

Islamic tradition relates that Muhammad received his first revelation in the Cave of Hira during one of his isolated retreats to the mountains. Thereafter, he received revelations over a period of 23 years. According to hadith and Muslim history, after Muhammad immigrated to Medina and formed an independent Muslim community, he ordered many of his companions to recite the Quran and to learn and teach the laws, which were revealed daily.

As it was initially spoken, the Quran was eventually recorded on tablets, bones, and the wide, flat ends of date palm fronds. Most suras were in use amongst early Muslims since they are mentioned in numerous sayings by both Sunni and Shia sources, relating Muhammad's use of the Quran as a call to Islam, the making of prayer, and the manner of recitation. However, the Quran did not exist in book form at the time of Muhammad's death in AD 632. There is agreement among scholars that Muhammad himself did not write down the revelation.

The first caliph, Abu Bakr (d. 634), subsequently decided to collect the writings in one volume so that it could be preserved. Zayd ibn Thabit (d. 655) was the person to collect the Quran since "he used to write the Divine Inspiration for Allah's Apostle." Thus, a group of scribes, most importantly Zayd, collected the verses and produced a handwritten manuscript of the complete book. The manuscript, according to Zayd, remained with Abu Bakr until he died.

Zayd's reaction to the task and the difficulties in collecting the Quranic material from parchments, palm-leaf stalks, thin stones (collectively known as suhuf), and from men who knew it by heart is recorded in earlier narratives. After Abu Bakr's death, Hafsa bint Umar, Muhammad's widow, was entrusted with the manuscript until the third caliph, Uthman ibn Affan, requested to make a copy.

In about AD 650, Uthman ibn Affan (d. 656), began noticing slight differences in pronunciation of the Quran as Islam expanded beyond the Arabian Peninsula into Persia, the Levant, and North Africa. In order to preserve the sanctity of the text, he ordered a committee headed by Zayd to use Abu Bakr's copy and prepare a standard copy of the Quran. Thus, within 20 years of Muhammad's death, the Quran was committed to written form. That text became the model from which copies were made and promulgated throughout the urban centers of the Muslim world. Other versions are believed to have been destroyed. The present form of the Quran text is accepted by Muslim scholars to be the original version compiled by Abu Bakr.

According to Shia, Ali ibn Abi Talib (d. 661) compiled a complete version of the Quran shortly after Muhammad's death. The order of this text differed from that gathered later during Uthman's era in that this version had been collected in chronological order. Despite this, he made no objection against the standardized Quran and accepted the Quran in circulation. Other personal copies of the Quran might have existed, including Ibn Mas'ud's and Ubay ibn Ka'b's codex, none of which exist today.

Critique: Muhammad's critics accuse him of being a possessed man, a soothsayer, or a magician since his experiences were similar to those claimed by such figures well known in ancient Arabia. Regarding the claim of divine origin, critics refer to preexisting sources, not only taken from the Bible, supposed to be older revelations of God, but also from heretic, apocryphal and Talmudic sources, such as The Syriac Infancy Gospel and Gospel of James. Due to the rejection of the Crucifixion of Jesus in the Quran, some scholars also suspect Manichaean influence, a dualistic religion believing in two eternal forces, having influences on the Quran. Christopher Hitchens states that Islam as a whole, both Hadith and the Quran, are little more than poorly structured plagiarisms, using earlier sacred works and traditions depending on what the situation seemed to require. Abrogation (Naskh) is often seen as an acknowledgment of contradicting Quranic verses. Other critics point at the negative moral attitude asserted by the Quran, such as commanding to strike disobedient wives, carnality in the afterlife, and commandments of warfare.

The verses which allegedly explain modern scientific facts about subjects such as biology, evolution of the earth, and human life, contain fallacies and are unscientific. Most claims of predictions rely on the ambiguity of the Arabic language. Despite calling itself a clear book, the Quranic language lacks clarity.

Counter: The Tafsir'ilmi believe the Quran predicts scientific knowledge, relating the author to non-human origin.

The Vedas
Founder: Vyasa compiled the Vedas, who arranged the four kinds of mantras into four Samhitas (Collections).

Location: Punjab, India
Date: 1500 and 1200 BC
Converts: 1.2 billion
Belief System:

- Pursue knowledge and understanding of the truth, the very essence of the universe and the only reality. According to the Vedas, truth is one, but the wise express it in a variety of ways.

- Believe in Brahma as the one true God who is formless, limitless, all-inclusive, and eternal. Brahma is not an abstract concept; it is a real entity that encompasses everything (seen and unseen) in the universe.

- The Vedas are Hindu scriptures that contain revelations received by ancient saints and sages. Hindus believe that the Vedas are without beginning and without end. When everything in the universe is destroyed (at the end of a cycle of time), the Vedas remain.

- Dharma helps in understanding the Hindu faith. It can be described as as right conduct, righteousness, moral law, and duty. Anyone who makes dharma central to one's life strives to do the right thing, according to one's duty and abilities, at all times.

- Believes that the individual soul (Atman) is neither created nor destroyed. It has been, it is, and it will be. Actions of the soul while residing in a body require that it reap the consequences of those actions in the next life, that is, the same soul in a different body. The kind of body the soul inhabits next is determined by Karma (actions accumulated in previous lives).

- Moksha is the soul's release from the cycle of death and rebirth. It occurs when the soul unites with Brahma by realizing its true nature. Several paths can lead to this realization and unity: the path of duty, the path of knowledge, and the path of devotion or unconditional surrender to God.

Summary:

There are four Vedas ("what is heard"): the Rigveda, the Yajurveda, the Samaveda, and the Atharvaveda. Each Veda has four subdivisions – the Samhitas (mantras and benedictions), the Aranyakas (text on rituals, ceremonies, sacrifices, and symbolic-sacrifices), the Brahmanas (commentaries on rituals, ceremonies, and sacrifices), and the Upanishads (texts discussing meditation, philosophy, and spiritual knowledge). Some scholars add a fifth category – the Upasanas (worship).

The Vedas have been orally transmitted since the 2nd millennium BC with the help of elaborate mnemonic techniques. The mantras, the oldest part of the Vedas, are recited today for their phonology rather than the semantics and are considered to be "primordial rhythms of creation," preceding the forms to which they refer. By reciting them, the cosmos is regenerated "by enlivening and nourishing the forms of creation at their base."

Rigveda: The Rigveda Samhita is the oldest surviving text. It is a collection of 1,028 Vedic Sanskrit hymns and 10,600 verses in all, organized into ten books. The hymns are dedicated to Rigvedic deities. The books were composed by poets from different priestly groups over the period between 1500 BC and 1200 BC in the Punjab (Sapta Sindhu) region of the northwest Indian subcontinent.

According to Michael Witzel, the initial codification took place at the end of the Rigvedic period at ca. 1200 BC, in the early Kuru kingdom.

Samaveda: The Samaveda Samhita consists of 1,549 stanzas, taken almost entirely (except for 75 mantras) from the Rigveda. While its earliest parts are believed to date from as early as the Rigvedic period, the existing compilation dates from the post-Rigvedic Mantra period of Vedic Sanskrit, between 1200 BC and 1000 BC or "slightly later," roughly contemporary with the Atharvaveda and the Yajurveda.

Yajurveda: The Yajurveda Samhita consists of prose mantras. It is a compilation of ritual offering formulas that were said by a priest while an individual performed ritual actions, such as those done before the yajna fire. The core text of the Yajurveda falls within the classical Mantra period of Vedic Sanskrit at the end of 2000 BC. Witzel dates the Yajurveda hymns to the early Indian Iron Age, after 1200 BC, and before 800 BC.

Atharvaveda: The Artharvaveda Samhita is the text belonging to the Atharvan and Angirasa poets. It has about 760 hymns, and about 160 of the hymns are in common with the Rigveda. Most of the verses are metrical, but some sections are in prose. The Atharvaveda was not considered as a Veda in the Vedic era, but was accepted as a Veda in late 1st millennium BC. It was compiled last, probably around 900 BC, although some of its material may go back to the time of the Rigveda or earlier.

Critique: Hinduism is a complex religion. It is as complex as the human mind. It is complex because Hinduism has a long history and, throughout its record, has adopted many different positional aspects into its religion. In fact, Hinduism is many religions in one. In this process, it has adopted several different, sometimes opposed schools of thought. The Advaita, for example, suggests that God's spirit and human spirit are not distinct, and therefore whoever gains insight into the depths of his own nature will also realize his identity with God and thereby reach salvation. The Dvaita, on the other hand, holds that the human spirit is not identical to God's, but it is dependent on Him, and therefore salvation depends on the cultivation of love for God and on God's grace. Within these opposed schools of thought, there are many philosophies, such as the personal God (Ishvara), the celestial beings that preside over the forces of nature and act as a link between God and humans (Nyaya), and the sovereign rulers of the forces of nature which govern under a supreme God (Mimamsa). Certain denominations of Hinduism (Vaishnavism or Smartism) even believe that from time to time, God comes to Earth as a human being to help humans along in their struggle toward enlightenment and salvation.

Hinduism, in general, is a self-help philosophy with the main objective to achieve a heightened spiritual experience. This is obtained through the following objectives: obligations and ethical tasks (Dharma), rebirth (Samsara), correct acts (Karma), and salvation (Moksha). Because Hinduism is several religions in one, each of the opinion streams deserves a separate critique, which would become tedious. The case in point is the concept of self-improvement. Hinduism believes salvation is obtained by a combination of predetermined factors associated with soul purification by multiple births and by personal discipline and disposition associated with Karma and Dharma. In other words, there is a portion of ourselves and of our destiny that we have no control over, but there are other aspects of our existence that we do have control and even have an obligation to control. This is baffling.

The Judeo-Christian Bible
The Hebrew Bible or Old Testament
Founder: God first revealed himself to a man named Abram
Location: Haran, present-day Turkey
Date: 2075 BC
Converts: 15 million
Belief System:

- Believe there is only one God who has established a covenant with them.
- Believe that God communicates to believers through prophets and rewards good deeds while also punishes evil.
- Most Jews (with the exception of a few groups) believe that their Messiah has not yet come but will one day.
- Jewish people worship in holy places known as synagogues, and their spiritual leaders are called rabbis.

Summary:

The Jewish sacred text is called the Tanakh or the "Hebrew Bible." It includes the same books as the Old Testament in the Christian Bible, but they're placed in a slightly different order. The Torah, the first five books of the Tanakh, outlines laws for Jews to follow. It's sometimes also referred to as the Pentateuch. The Hebrew names of the five books in the Torah are derived from the first words in the respective texts, and are the following: Genesis (Beresheeth), Exodus (Shemot), Leviticus (Vayikra), Numbers (Bamidbar), and Deuteronomy (Devarim).

The first eleven chapters of Genesis provide accounts of the creation (or ordering) of the world and the history of God's early relationship with humanity. The remaining thirty-nine chapters provide an account of God's covenant with the biblical patriarchs Abraham, Isaac, Jacob (also called Israel), and Jacob's children, the "Children of Israel," especially Joseph. Tells how God commanded Abram (b. 2150 BC) to leave his family and home in the city of Ur of Chaldeans and settle in the land of Canaan, and how the Children of Israel later moved to Egypt. The remaining four books of the Torah tell the story of Moses, who was in the scene 600 years after the patriarchs (1527 – 1407 BC). He leads the Children of Israel from slavery in ancient Egypt (1447 BC) to the renewal of their covenant with God at biblical Mount Sinai and their wanderings in the desert until a new generation was ready to enter the land of Canaan. The Torah ends with the death of Moses.

The Ten Commandments in the Torah provide the basis for Jewish religious law. Jewish tradition also established 613 rules (taryag mitzvot). The rest of the books in the Tanakh include: Nevi'im, Ketuvim, and other books.

Nevi'im: ("Prophets") or "prophets", is the second main division of the Tanakh. It contains two sub-groups; the Former Prophets (Nevi'im Rishonim, the narrative books of Joshua, Judges, Samuel, and Kings) and the Latter Prophets (Nevi'im Aharonim, that include the books of Isaiah, Jeremiah and Ezekiel and the Twelve Minor Prophets). The Nevi'im tell the story of the rise of the Hebrew monarchy and its division into two kingdoms, ancient Israel and Judah, It focuses on the conflicts between the Israelites and other nations, and the conflicts among Israelites, specifically, struggles between believers in "the LORD God" (Yahweh) and believers in foreign gods. Also, on the criticism of unethical and unjust behavior of Israelite elites and rulers; in which prophets played a crucial and leading role. It ends with the conquest of the Kingdom of Israel by the Assyrians (772 BC), followed by the conquest of the Kingdom of Judah by the Babylonians and the destruction of the Temple in Jerusalem (586 BC).

Former Prophets: are the books Joshua, Judges, Samuel, and Kings. They contain narratives that begin immediately after the death of Moses with the divine appointment of Joshua as his successor, who then leads the people of Israel into the Promised Land (1355 BC), and end with the release from imprisonment of the last king of Judah.

Latter Prophets: are divided into two groups, the "major" prophets, Isaiah, Jeremiah, Ezekiel, Daniel, and the Twelve Minor Prophets, collected into a single book. The collection is broken up to form twelve individual books in the Christian Old Testament: Hosea (Hoshea), Joel (Yoel), Amos (Amos), Obadiah (Ovadyah), Jonah (Yonah), Micah (Mikhah), Nahum (Nahum), Habakkuk (Havakuk), Zephaniah (Tsefanya), Haggai (Khagay), Zechariah (Zekharyah), and Malachi (Malakhi).

Ketuvim: or "writings," is the third and final section of the Tanakh. The Ketuvim are believed to have been written under the Ruach HaKodesh (the Holy Spirit) but with one level less authority than that of prophecy. In Masoretic manuscripts (and some printed editions), Psalms, Proverbs, and Job are presented in a special two-column form emphasizing the parallel stitches in the verses, which are a function of their poetry. Collectively, these three books are known as Sifrei Emet (an acronym of the titles in Hebrew that yields Emet which is also the Hebrew for "truth").

The five relatively short books of Song of Songs, Book of Ruth, the Book of Lamentations, Ecclesiastes, and Book of Esther are collectively known as the Hamesh Megillot. These are the latest books collected and designated as "authoritative" in the Jewish canon even though they were not completed until the 2nd century AD.

Other books: The remaining books in Ketuvim are Daniel, Ezra–Nehemiah, and Chronicles. Their narratives all openly describe relatively late events (i.e., the Babylonian captivity and the subsequent restoration of Zion). The Talmudic tradition ascribes late authorship to all of them. Two of them (Daniel and Ezra) are the only books in the Tanakh with significant portions in Aramaic.

Canonization: The Ketuvim is the last of the three portions of the Tanakh to have been accepted as biblical canon. While the Torah may have been considered canon by Israel as early as the 5th century BC and the Former and Latter Prophets were canonized by the 2nd century BC, the Ketuvim was not a fixed canon until the 2nd century AD. Evidence suggests, however, that the people of Israel were adding what would become the Ketuvim to their holy literature shortly after the canonization of the prophets. As early as 132 BC, references suggest that the Ketuvim was starting to take shape, although it lacked a formal title. References in the four Gospels, as well as other books of the New Testament, indicate that many of these texts were both commonly known and counted as having some degree of religious authority early in the 1st century AD.

Original languages

The Tanakh was mainly written in biblical Hebrew, with some small portions (Ezra 4:8–6:18 and 7:12–26, Jeremiah 10:11, Daniel 2:4–7:28) written in biblical Aramaic, a sister language which became the lingua franca for much of the Semitic world.

The Septuagint, is a translation of the Hebrew Scriptures and some related texts into koine Greek, which begun in the late 3rd century BC and completed by 132 BC, initially in Alexandria, but in time it was completed elsewhere as well. The Septuagint is the basis for the Old Latin, Slavonic, Syriac, Old Armenian, Old Georgian, and Coptic versions of the Christian Old Testament. The Roman Catholic and Eastern Orthodox Churches use most of the books of the Septuagint, while Protestant churches usually do not. After the Protestant Reformation, many Protestant Bibles began to follow the Jewish canon and exclude the additional texts, which came to be called biblical apocrypha. The Apocrypha are included under a separate heading in the King James Version of the Bible, the basis for the Revised Standard Version.

The New Testament

Founder: God sent His begotten son Jesus as His Messiah (Christ)

Location: Galilee and Jerusalem, present-day Israel

Date: AD 30-33

Converts: 2.4 billion

Belief System:

- Believe there's only one God, creator of the heavens and the earth.

- Believe that God consists of three personages: the Father (God himself), the son Jesus, and the Holy Spirit.
- Believe that Jesus fulfills all the prophecies about the Messiah in the Old Testament.
- Believe that Jesus was born of a virgin, lived a sinless life, sacrificed Himself for the sins of the world, and on the third day was resurrected.
- Believe that after appearing to His disciples for 40 days, Jesus ascended to heaven to return at the end times, as is prophesied.

Summary:

The New Testament is the name given to the second and final portion of the Christian Bible. Jesus is its central figure. The term "New Testament" came into use in the 2nd century during a controversy among Christians over whether the Hebrew Bible should be included with the Christian writings as sacred scripture. The New Testament presupposes the inspiration of the Old Testament.

The New Testament is a collection of 27 books of 4 different genres of Christian literature (four Gospels, one account of the Acts of the Apostles, 21 Epistles, and Revelation or Apocalypse). The mainstream consensus is that the New Testament was written in a form of koine Greek, which was the common language of the Eastern Mediterranean from the Conquests of Alexander the Great (335–323 BC) until the evolution of Byzantine Greek (c. 600).

The original autographs, that is, the original Greek writings and manuscripts written by the original authors of the New Testament, have not survived. But historically, copies exist of those original autographs, transmitted and preserved in a number of manuscripts. There have been some minor variations, additions, or omissions, in some of the texts. When ancient scribes copied earlier books, they sometimes wrote notes on the margins of the page (marginal glosses) to correct their text – especially if a scribe accidentally omitted a word or line – and also to comment about the text. When later scribes were copying the copy, they were sometimes uncertain which notes were intended to be included as part of the text.

Development of the Christian Canons: The Old Testament canon entered into Christian use with the Greek Septuagint translations. In addition, various writings were added that would become the New Testament. In the 4th century, a series of synods (a council convened to decide an issue of doctrine, administration, or application) which decided the canon of the Old Testament and the New Testament that is used until today, most notably the Synod of Hippo in 393 AD. Also, c. 400, Jerome produced a definitive Latin edition of the Bible (the Latin Vulgate).

Divine inspiration: The Second Epistle to Timothy says that "all scripture is given by inspiration of God, and is profitable for doctrine, for reproof, for correction, for instruction in righteousness" (2 Timothy 3:16). Various related but distinguishable views on divine inspiration include:

- the view of the Bible as the inspired Word of God - the belief that God, through the Holy Spirit, intervened and influenced the words, message, and collation of the Bible

- the view that the Bible is also infallible and incapable of error in matters of faith and practice, but not necessarily in historic or scientific matters
- the view that the Bible represents the inerrant Word of God, without error in any aspect, spoken by God and written down in its perfect form by humans

Within these broad beliefs, many schools of hermeneutics (the branch of knowledge that deals with interpretation) operate. "Bible scholars claim that discussions about the Bible must be put into its context within church history and then into the context of contemporary culture." Fundamentalist Christians believe the doctrine of biblical literalism, where the Bible is not only inerrant, but the meaning of the text is clear to the average reader (e.g., does not require an intermediary).

Critique: Biblical archaeology is the archaeology that relates to and sheds light upon the Hebrew Scriptures and the Christian Greek Scriptures (or the New Testament). It is used to help determine the lifestyle and practices of people living in biblical times. There are a wide range of interpretations in the field of biblical archaeology. One broad division includes biblical maximalism, which generally takes the view that most of the Old Testament (the Hebrew Bible) is based on history, although it is presented through the religious viewpoint of its time. It is considered to be the opposite of biblical minimalism, which considers the Bible to be a purely post-exilic (5th century BC and later) composition. Even among those scholars who adhere to biblical minimalism, the Bible is a historical document containing first-hand information on the Hellenistic and Roman eras, and there is universal scholarly consensus that the events of the 6th century BC Babylonian captivity have a basis in history.

The historicity of the biblical account of the history of ancient Israel and Judah of the 10th to 7th centuries BC is disputed in scholarship. The biblical account of the 8th to 7th centuries BC is widely, but not universally, accepted as historical, while the verdict on the earliest period of the United Monarchy (10th century BC) and the historicity of David is unclear. The biblical account of events of the Exodus from Egypt in the Torah and the migration to the Promised Land and the period of Judges are not considered historical in scholarship.

Counter: Archeology cannot "prove" the Bible is true. But archeology has provided exciting and dramatic confirmation of the Bible's accuracy. Here just a few of the hundreds of examples:

- In 1947, shepherds stumbled upon a cave in a rugged, arid area on the western side of the Dead Sea. What they discovered inside was soon proclaimed the greatest archaeological find of the 20th century. Over the next few years, other similar remote caves in the area were found. The caves contained over 800 fragmentary documents, mainly consisting of Hebrew writings on leather (with a few on parchment), including fragments of 190 biblical scrolls. Most of these are small, containing no more than one-tenth of a book; however, a complete Isaiah scroll has been found. Almost every Old Testament book is present, and there are also other writings valued by the community that inhabited in the vicinity of those caves.

It appears the earliest scrolls date to the mid-3rd century BC, and most to the 1st or 2nd centuries BC.

- Perhaps the greatest contribution of this find is to our understanding of the transmission of the biblical text. It is encouraging to note that the differences are minimal between the Old Testament texts of the Dead Sea Scrolls (written between 300 and 100 BC) and the various editions of the Hebrew texts produced a thousand years later and used today. The meaning of the text itself is not affected by these differences.

- In 1868, a missionary in Jerusalem found a stone tablet for sale that appeared to be from ancient times. The sellers broke the tablet into a number of pieces to sell them one at a time to make more money. Fortunately, a copy of the tablet was made prior to the break (this copy is in the Louvre today). On the tablet is a text written in Moabite dating to the 9th century BC. It was perhaps a victory stone erected by King Mesha to commemorate his military achievements. The text begins, "I am Mesha, son of Chemosh, king of Moab."

- Prominent in the text is the king's version of a war fought with Israel in 850 BC, in which Moab revolted against King Jehoram of the northern kingdom of Israel soon after the death of Ahab. Of particular interest is that the Bible records the same incident in 2 Kings 3. The two accounts differ in perspective. Mesha emphasizes his victories over Israel in capturing cities under Israelite control. The biblical writer, to the contrary, highlights Israel's successful counter-attacks against the Moabites.

- At one time, scholars thought that Luke (author of Luke's Gospel) was entirely wrong regarding the events surrounding the birth of Jesus (Luke 2:1-3). Critics argued that there was no census, that Quirinius was not governor of Syria at that time, and that everyone did not have to return to his ancestral home for these events. But archeological discoveries show that the Romans had a regular enrollment of taxpayers and also held censuses every fourteen years. This procedure began under Augustus. Further, we find that Quirinius was, indeed, governor of Syria around 7 BC. It is supposed that he was governor twice, once in 7 BC and again in 6 AD (the date ascribed by Josephus). A papyrus found in Egypt gives instructions for the conduct of a census.

- In some cases, Luke's usages of certain words were criticized by skeptics. For example, Luke refers to Philippi as a "district" of Macedonia (Acts 16:12) by using the Greek word "meris." Some argued that meris referred to a "portion," not a "district." Archaeological excavations, however, have shown that this very word was used to describe the divisions of the district.

- Still, another case is Luke's usage of politarchs to denote the civil authorities of Thessalonica (Acts 17:6-8). Since politarch is not found in the classic literature, Luke was again assumed to be wrong. However, some nineteen inscriptions that make use of that title have been found. Interestingly enough, five of these are in reference to the city of Thessalonica. One of the inscriptions was discovered in a Roman arch at Thessalonica, and in it are found the names of six of that city's politarchs.

- In 1961, an inscription was found on a damaged stone column which confirms not only the rule of Pilate in

Judea but also his preference for the title 'Prefect.' In Latin, the inscription (dated to 26-37 AD) reads:

TIBERIEUM
IUS PILATUS
ECTUS IUDA
Translated, this reads: "To Tiberius – [Pont]ius Pilate, [Pref]ect of Judea."

Analysis of the Writings

After reading these excerpts of the writings that claim to be the Word of God, I ask you again, which one covers all the bases with respect to:

- Being ancient – covering important portions of human spiritual history, explaining how everything got created, why we sin, how to get back into good graces with God (or how to be forgiven) – The Book of Mormon is definitely not ancient as it was written in 1823. The Koran, even though was written in the 4th century AD, cannot be considered ancient. The Vedas and the Bible, having been written in 1500 BC, are considered ancient texts.
- Being credible – describing supernatural events but not fantasies or involving mythological beings – The Book of Mormon clearly tells an incredible story full of fantasies. The Koran and the history surrounding it include many supernatural events but remains in the credible realm. The Vedas are full of mythology. The Bible is full of supernatural events, but the personages are real people with human flaws and in the story remains in the credible realm as well.
- Which one makes more sense?
- Which one would you deposit your faith in?

Summarizing, let us put our findings in a table for clarity:

Writing	Ancient?	Credible?	Makes Sense?	Deposit Faith?
Mormon	No	No	No	No
The Koran	No	Yes	No	No
The Vedas	Yes	No	No	No
The Bible	Yes	Yes	Yes	Yes

This factual analysis, using logic in the absence of tradition and sentimentalities, points to the only true Word of God. This writing must then contain the fundamental truths about ourselves and about God and His plans for us. Another factor pointing at the Bible as *the* Word of God is the important fact that Jesus is the only Messiah who claims to be God. This is a fact that cannot be overlooked. In fact, it is essential to the discussion. If we had two or more historical figures who claimed to be God, then we would have to expand the analysis to discern who is really the Messiah. But since we only have one claiming to be God, and it comes from the story we have determined that checks all the prerequisites needed to deposit our faith in, then the Bible is *the* actual Word of God, and Jesus *is* the Messiah.

What the Bible says

The Bible's first words are (Gen. 1:1): "In the beginning God created the heavens and the earth." If you believe that first phrase is true, you should not have any problem believing the rest of the story. The story covers relevant parts of the history of humankind, but it is not a description of the history of mankind. It only covers what is relevant to the message God has for us, which can be summarized as this: 'I created you, I gave you a simple rule, you disobeyed, disobedience has a consequence, the consequence is that now you have to deal with sin, sin always leads to physical death, but I love you so much that I will provide a way for you to obtain eternal life under My comfort, as was My original plan, if only you believe in what I say and on My promise. I know you are incredulous, so my word will include in many instances predictions of what will happen in the future in order that you recognize that I AM who I claim to be.'

The first five books of the Old Testament were compiled by Moses, who led the Jews out of slavery in Egypt. The journey is well documented and witnessed by about 2 million people. Besides, there are over 100 references in the books written after this migration story and the miraculous events that occurred during that journey. Archeological digs keep finding the places mentioned in Exodus and cannot refute the supernatural events that took place. It starts with the book of Genesis which tells the story of creation, how Adam and Eve disobeyed God's only restriction in Paradise; to not eat the fruits of the Tree of Knowledge of Good and Evil. Their disobedience established the sinful nature of all human beings descended from them. It tells the story of Noah and the flood, the lives of Abraham, Isaac, Jacob, and Joseph, and how a family of believers in God became a nation after 430 years in Egypt.

Exodus tells the story of the Jews' journey out of Egypt and into the desert and God's instructions to build the Tabernacle. Leviticus describes God's instructions about making offerings and how to conduct themselves while camped around the Tabernacle. Numbers describes the receiving of the Law, the murmurs of the people against Moses and his brother Levi, and the Jews' poor confidence in God when they were just outside the Promised Land. Deuteronomy recaps the 40 years of wilderness wanderings and the need to observe the Law before being allowed to finally enter the Promised Land.

The following seven books describe the early history of the Israelites in the Middle East (Joshua, Judges, Ruth, Samuel I and II, and Kings I and II).

The two books of Chronicles highlight the important events of each king of Israel and Judah (the kingdom was split after the death of Salomon into the ten northern tribes forming the kingdom of Israel, and the two southern tribes which formed the kingdom of Judah).

The sixteen books of the Prophets provide the impossible standard to match by any other religious story. The Bible sets the mark high by giving predictions of future events. How do we know who was telling the truth? There were hundreds of self-proclaimed prophets who provided advice to the kings when matters boiled down to choice or when they deviated from the truth. The reason the prophets we now find in the Bible are there was because they proved their statement "according to Jehovah" was true. That is, their prophesies were proven.

Each prophet of God had near-time prophesies (within a few months or years), and far-time prophesies (much later, beyond the prophet's life). If they predicted the near-time prophesies and these occurred, the chances were high that all the prophesies they had given were true, and God was truly speaking through them. Some prophesies were fulfilled just recently, like the creation of the state of Israel on May 14, 1948 (Eze 36:24, 37:12, 37:21), and others are still to come, like the war of Armageddon (Rev 16:16, 39:11). For example, the prophet Jeremiah (29:10), in about 600 BC, prophesied that the Jews would be invaded by the Babylonians (which occurred within his lifetime in 586 BC), and that they would suffer exile for 70 years because they disobeyed the Law. After this period, they would be allowed to return to their land. Cyrus the Great of Persia decreed and financed the rebuilding of the Temple in 536 BC and Jews began the long and difficult process of returning to their land.

Daniel (9:24-25), who lived in Babylon after his deportation in about 586 BC, prophesied the date of the Anointed One (the Messiah's) triumphal entrance into Jerusalem as being 69 x 7 = 483 lunar years or 476 calendar years after the order to rebuild Jerusalem was given, which occurred March 14, 445 BC by Artaxerxes I of Persia. The difference between these dates is April 6, AD 32, the date Jesus entered Jerusalem on a donkey! In fact, Daniel's following verse (9:26) prophesied not only Jesus' death, but the future destruction of Jerusalem and the Temple "… the

Anointed One will be killed, appearing to have accomplished nothing, and a ruler will arise whose armies will destroy the city and the Temple." This destruction occurred in AD 70 under the Roman emperor Titus Flavius Vespasianus.

Malachi (3:1), in 460 BC, wrote the last book in the Old Testament and also ends with a prophesy of the long-awaited Messiah, but it is not after about 489 years that John the Baptist begins to prepare the way for the appearance of Jesus in the scene. There are 333 prophesies about Jesus in the Old Testament and only 109 of them have been fulfilled by His first coming. Even though there are references of Him suffering for our sins like a lamb of God placed as a sacrifice, it also describes Him as conquering and establishing a new kingdom in Israel. The prophesies, maybe on purpose to test our faith, did not specify that this process was going to take place in two separate events with a lot of time in between.

So, based on the analysis above, in order to talk about God, it requires you to be familiar with the entire Bible. It is a fascinating book. I do not know why people have no issue reading Tolstoy's "War and Peace" but cringe at the idea of reading the Bible. It is the story that describes why we are sinners, how God chooses a person and promises him that the generations after him would be very numerous, how a family of twelve brothers become a nation in Egypt, how that nation, after they became enslaved by the Egyptians, was guided and protected by God and emigrated to the Promised Land, how on their way there they are given the Ten Commandments, how the Law was the mirror that reflected the people's own sinfulness, how prophecies specified a temporary exile in the future and also the coming of a Messiah that would save them from their sins and culminating with the birth of Jesus and the Gospel of the Good News.

Why "good news" you may ask? Well, before Jesus makes His appearance in history, humanity was doomed. All cultures and empires in the world were idolaters, except the Jews (at times). The whole point of God creating the nation of Israel was to use them as an example, a beacon of light among the existing spiritual darkness, for the rest of the world to see that a monotheistic belief system was in favor with God, as shown by allowing them to thrive supernaturally to greatness against all odds while surrounded by numerous enemies. As always, God conditions His favor with obeyance.

In spite of many warnings that the prophets gave in name of God, the Jews did eventually forget the Commandments and stopped worshiping God. As a result, they were invaded and the survivors were taken captives for a foretold prescribed time, after which the Temple and the city of Jerusalem were rebuilt. After again a foretold number of years, Jesus enters Jerusalem, but the religious authorities did not receive Him as King and Lord. They, in fact, plotted to kill Him. The people who did hail Him as King and Lord when He was riding a young donkey down the road from the Mount of Olives while shouting "Hosanna!" while spreading garments and leafy branches ahead of Him, turned on Him a few days later and shouted, "Crucify Him!" This failure to recognize Jesus as the Messiah caused the city and the Temple to be completely destroyed and the Jews to be wholly exiled for 1,878 years.

But all of this was in God's plans because the outcome of this tragedy was that in the following 280 years, most of the world changed from polytheistic idolaters to monotheistic Christians.

Even today in the 21st century, we continue to hail Jesus as Lord, although mostly unconsciously, by writing the date of every day, since our current calendar specifies the day and year that He was born. Every day we look at a calendar or write the day's date, we remember how many years it has been since His birth.

God's Covenants with His People

God made different pacts with people over time. People set in their ways are difficult to change, especially in the spiritual realm. Change had to be achieved in baby steps, thus the progression in the covenants God made with people. When God first spoke to Abram, all peoples (including Abram) were idolaters and polytheists. God convinced Abram to leave his family and native country and go to a land He was going to lead him to and make of him a great nation. God promised Abram he was going to be blessed and would be a blessing to many. In fact, God promised Abram (Gen. 12:3) that "all families on earth will be blessed through you." God's covenant or pact with Abram (meaning exalted father), who He later renamed Abraham (meaning father of many), was the extent of the land promised (Gen. 15:18): "I have given this land to your descendants, all the way from the border of (the brook of) Egypt to the great Euphrates River."

God's second covenant was with Moses on Mount Sinai when the Ten Commandments were given to the Israelites, now converted into a nation. "After four generations, your descendants will return here to this land," God promised Abraham (Gen. 15:16). This covenant had a physical or social component and a spiritual component, both needed for the transformation of people. The social component has to do with the introduction of the Law. The law creates necessary behavior boundaries essential for an orderly and productive society. The spiritual component has to do with the law acting as a mirror on which people realize that they are imperfect, that they are sinners. Without the Law, how can you know you are at fault? The Law defines sin.

God had promised a specific land, then provided the Law so that society could function, and people would realize how sinful they really were. Next, God provided the means to fulfill Jeremiah's (31:33) prediction: "I will put My law in their minds, and write it on their hearts, and I will be their God, and they shall be My people." In other words, people will no longer comply with the law only for fear of God, but they will do so because they love Him. To fulfill that, God sends His only son Jesus to make a new covenant; to sacrifice Himself to pay for all sins in exchange for a confession of sins and profession of faith. This is what Jesus said according to Matthew (26:26-28) during the Last Supper as He was breaking bread: "Take this and eat it, for this is My body" and then while sharing wine with His disciples: "Each of you drink from it, for this is My blood, which confirms the new covenant between God and His people. It is poured out as a sacrifice to forgive the sins of many."

Conclusion

To discuss religion, it is necessary to shift the discussion to God and, by natural progression, to the writings of God. Only four religions claim that their version of *the* truth comes from God. Logical analysis of these writings indicate that only the Bible checks all the requirements necessary to be considered *the* Word of God.

Furthermore, Jesus fulfils all the requirements and the predictions made in the Old Testament (the Hebrew portion of the Bible) and is the only Messiah that *claims* to be God.

Going back to "being good" or "doing more good than evil" as not being good enough in God's eyes is explained by the fact that God does not gauge sins. All sin is awful and inadmissible to God, and therefore we all are deserving death. However, if we accept Jesus into our hearts as our Lord and Savior, God no longer sees our sins because He sees Jesus' pure spirit in our stead.

Do Politics and God Ever Converge?

In the current age of mindless "separation of church and state," this question is important and critical. You may ask, is that not part of our US Constitution to have this separation? Curiously, I will have to respond; no, it never was. I will invite the Constitution, some of the authors, and history to witness for this argument.

The First Amendment to the US Constitution says: "Congress shall make no law respecting an establishment of religion; or prohibiting the free exercise thereof; or abridging the freedom of speech, or of the press, or the right of the people peaceably to assemble, and to petition the Government for a redress of grievances." For 171 years of the country's existence there was little debate over the meaning of "Congress shall make no law respecting an *establishment* of religion."

Roger Williams, founder of Rhode Island, was the first public official to opine in 1644 that an authentic Christian church would only be possible if there was "a wall or hedge of separation" between the "wilderness of the world" and "the garden of the church." Williams believed that any government involvement in the church would corrupt it. He is actually making the argument contrary to today's tenet. He wanted to keep politics out of the church, which I agree completely.

Thomas Jefferson, in his 1802 letter to the Danbury Baptist Association, wrote, "I contemplate with sovereign reverence that act of the whole American people which declared that their legislature should 'make no law respecting an establishment of religion, or prohibiting the free exercise thereof,' thus building a wall of separation between Church & State." Though not explicitly stated in the First Amendment, the clause is *currently* interpreted to mean that the Constitution requires the separation of church and state. Nothing can be further from the truth. It is clear what Thomas Jefferson means in his famous letter; that the legislature (Congress) should never establish a *particular* State religion for the country. That this wall of separation between Church and State was meant to *protect* its citizens from the State *establishing* and *imposing* a specific religion.

For 171 years, the American people and politicians understood it as written by Thomas Jefferson and had no quarrels with it. As the citizenry became more diverse and faith became more dispersed with other faiths or even became null, challenges arose to existing laws and practices, and eventually, the Supreme Court was called upon to determine the meaning of that First Amendment clause. What follows is a list of choice cases dealing with *separation of church and state.* The subsequent references to the "establishment clause" means "Congress shall make no law respecting an establishment of religion":

- In Everson v. Board of Education (1947), the Court held that the establishment clause is one of the liberties protected by the due process clause of the Fourteenth Amendment, making it applicable to *state laws* and *local ordinances.* Since that "can of worms" was opened, the process of separation of church and state, as interpreted today, began.

- In Lemon v. Kurtzman (1971), the Court established a three-pronged test for laws dealing with religious establishment. To be constitutional, a statute must have "a secular legislative purpose," it must have principal effects that neither advance nor inhibit religion, and it must not foster "an excessive government entanglement with religion."
- In 1971, the Court also considered the constitutionality of a Pennsylvania statute that provided financial support to nonpublic (private religious) schools for teacher salaries, textbooks, and instructional materials for secular subjects; and a Rhode Island statute that provided direct supplemental salary payments to teachers in private religious elementary schools.
- Justice Sandra Day O'Connor proposed an endorsement test that asks whether a particular government action amounts to an endorsement of religion. In Lynch v. Donnelly (1984), O'Connor noted that the establishment clause prohibits the government from making adherence to a religion relevant to a person's standing in the political community. Her fundamental concern was whether government action conveyed a message to non-adherents that they are outsiders. The endorsement test is often invoked in religious display cases.
- In County of Allegheny v. American Civil Liberties Union (1989), a group of justices led by Justice Anthony M. Kennedy in his dissent developed a coercion test: the government does not violate the establishment clause unless it provides direct aid to religion in a way that would tend to establish a state church or involve citizens in religion against their will.

- Questions involving appropriate use of government funds are increasingly subject to the neutrality test, which requires the government to treat religious groups the same as it would any other similarly situated group. In a test of Ohio's school voucher program, the Court held 5-4 in Zelman v. Simmons-Harris (2002), that Ohio's program is part of the state's general, neutral undertaking to provide educational opportunities to children and does not violate the establishment clause. In his opinion for the majority, Chief Justice William H. Rehnquist wrote that the "Ohio program is entirely neutral with respect to religion."

- In McCreary County v. American Civil Liberties Union (2005), the Court ruled that the display of the Ten Commandments in two Kentucky courtrooms was unconstitutional but refused in the companion case, Van Orden v. Perry (2005), to require the removal of a long-standing monument to the Ten Commandments on the grounds of the Texas State Capitol.

The US Declaration of Independence and Constitution are a rare attempt by humanity to unite or connect the physical life in society (politics) with the spiritual life (God). For this, God has blessed this country with prosperity unequal to any other country in the world, while its citizens and institutions recognized and trusted in God. They did this for 171 years. The legal interpretations of the last 74 years have been removing, little by little, this Godly infusion in the US Constitution through state laws and local ordinances that are undermining it. As a result, evil is beginning to rear its ugly face.

What Does the Bible Say About These Times?

About 3,000 years ago, Israel was ruled by Judges. But the Israelites in those times had poor faith. Most were lured by the barbaric customs and the idolatry of the surrounding kingdoms, which oppressed them. When things got really bad, they would cry out to God for deliverance, and God would send them a "judge" or leader to obtain victory over their enemies. After a while, the cycle would repeat. The Israelites did not seem to learn that when they forget God and His Commandments, their enemies began to oppress them again. This situation can be described with the following verse (Judges 17:6): "In those days Israel had no King; all the people did whatever seemed *right* in their *own* eyes." This verse is applicable to our situation today.

In our days, we have no King. At the time of the judges, the King for the Israelites was God. In our days, a lot of people do not believe in God. Without God, we have no protection against evil. The devil is constantly lurking for signs of weakness to oppress us. Weakness is having poor faith in God. "... faith comes by hearing, and hearing by the Word of God," says the apostle Paul (Rom. 10:17). Therefore, we can obtain faith by actually reading the Word of God. In Isaiah 1:18 (KJV), God says: "Come now and let us reason together..." God is reasonable. He is our Father, our Creator. He loves us. As a loving father, He wants the best for us. The apostle Matthew (7:11) transcribes the words of Jesus: "So if you, sinful people, know how to give good gifts to your children, how much more will your heavenly Father give good gifts to those who ask him?" Therefore, we just have to ask for faith while we read His word.

"All the people did whatever seemed right in their eyes." Without God, we end up doing what pleases us, not what pleases our King. Sin is pleasurable for a season, but when that time passes, we end up paying dearly. Either in this life with the consequences of our particular sin, after which hopefully (and often painfully), we repent and change to a faithful life, or in the afterlife when who knows what will happen, but the prospects are not good. For some reason, God wants us to confess and demonstrate that we love Him while we are in this earthly realm.

When we forget God, the enemy begins to oppress us. This oppression is not necessarily dramatic. In fact, it is often subtle and pleasant, but soon enough, our conscience tells us "this is not right," but we may keep falling for it. At one point, we either say "No!" or find an excuse or compromise to continue on that path that will lead us to destruction. Deep inside us, we know that is what will happen, but the lure is so strong.

What About Those Who Do Not Believe in God?

You may not believe that God exists, but what you do not realize is that to believe in anything else (e.g., Big Bang, Mother Nature, the Great Spirit, the Creative Force, etc.), requires more faith than required to believe in the God of the Bible. Take the Big Bang hypothesis, for example (the Big Bang is not a theory, it is a simple hypothesis, a theory is a proven and tested hypothesis, and the evidence for the Big Bang has not reached that level of proof in the scientific method). To believe that a primordial explosion created the galaxies, stars, and planets, one must believe that matter suddenly appeared from nothing and that it was densely compacted and spinning really fast, and that it all of a sudden exploded! So much matter cannot appear from nothing. Why was it spinning, and what made it spin? Why and how come it exploded? It is a lot easier to believe, "In the beginning God created…" But your mind is set; you believe in anything you are told that does not involve the Bible. Why? Because it makes you uneasy to measure up against a standard. You bought up into the pop culture that insinuates that there are no absolutes; that everything in life is painted in shades of gray. You equate God with the story of Santa Claus to infants. You believe in science, not fairytales, you tell yourself.

That desire to be free of norms is the driver for the popular movements that camouflage atheism, such as uniformitarianism (any change is slow), materialism (only material things matter), naturalism (anything natural is good), evolutionism (it is natural to be animals), and believe it or not, racism (only the strong survive). These movements have a subtle message but are slowly saturating our lives and are specially directed to our youth. Do you not believe it so? Ask yourself, why is it that only evolution is being taught in schools? I know, "separation of church and state." That pretext is so bogus. There is no such thing in the Constitution, and you know it. Thomas Jefferson simply sent in 1801 a letter to the Danbury Baptist Association of Connecticut discussing the separation of civil authority from ecclesiastical authority. That is, the state would never have an "official" religion. He never suggested that the state should separate from moral values. The proof is that up until the 1960s, the Bible was taught in public schools. And what happens when society moves away from moral standards? You get more violence, more crime, high divorce rates, more suicides, more drug use, etc. In other words, total degradation of society. Is that not happening today? If schools are supposed to prepare our youth for life in society, should not they be given at least all the information available? Is it not creationism another hypothesis and as credible as (if not more than) evolutionism? Why are you so afraid to be confronted with another plausible explanation for our existence?

There are other ways that the above movements are creeping into our lives. Consider the media. Religious people are portrayed as wackos, but philosophers, environmentalists, and sociologists are portrayed by the media as people who work for the betterment of society. The sciences, and, in particular, the scientific societies, are especially jealous against questioning evolutionism; they view it as progressive but will not allow the scientific method to properly test it. Scientists who dare question evolutionism are shunned from their societies and therefore are either prevented from getting funds to investigate further or never get through the necessary peer review to publish their findings.

In fact, as a fellow scientist, I believe evolutionism is, from its foundation, totally unscientific. Evolutionism was created by philosophers and spiritualists, a "scientific" faction that was looking for a "theory" in total opposition to the Bible. This process began in 1734 when Swedenborg, a philosopher, and spiritualist that wrote "Principia," a book that describes the creation of our Solar System from a nebula. Another philosopher, Comte de Buffon, shortly thereafter came up with the concept that the different species originated from one another. Lamarck, in 1809, wrote "Philosophie Zoologique," where he discusses the concept of inheritance of acquired characteristics and uniformitarianism. Chambers, a spiritualist, writes in 1844 "Vestiges of Creation," where he describes his ideas on evolution. Wallace in the mid-1800s conceives the idea of "survival of the fittest," but Darwin, a school dropout, with the help of Lyell, a geologist who described his hypothesis on sedimentary strata in 1833, pirated Wallace's material and published it in 1859 as "Origin of the Species by Means of Natural Selection or the Preservation of Favored Races." You read it right: "or the Preservation of Favored Races." I wonder on which side would the ACLU be if this book would have been published today. The foundation of evolutionism is totally unscientific (and racist). How did it become "scientific"?

To prove that evolutionism is an actual theory, it must be demonstrable in six major scientific areas: cosmic (it cannot prove who, what, and how was matter, space, and time created), chemical (it cannot explain how elements heavier than iron are created), stellar (it cannot explain why galaxies are still well-formed spirals), organic (it cannot explain how life started from inorganic ingredients), macro-evolution (it cannot explain how apparent simple organisms are so complex), and micro-evolution (it only explains how varieties of organisms evolved within the same kind). Of the six scientific areas, evolutionism can only explain one, which is obvious to everyone; that is; adaptation to the environment makes organisms change (e.g., wolves, foxes, to dogs). This adaptation is always along the same kind of organism, never across kinds, which is wrongly suggested by evolutionists.

The Achilles heel of evolution is how the geological data is being interpreted. The way that Lyell was able to make his hypothesis stick was to exclude all sudden and catastrophic geological events and to create a vast time scale for Earth's history. Of course, we see little change in our lifetime, unless one lives through a catastrophic event, such as a devastating earthquake, a flood, or a tsunami. Therefore, one can easily extrapolate our personal experience and conclude that an enormous amount of time is needed to cause the changes observed in nature. But we forget that numerous catastrophic events have occurred, some of which have been recorded either in written accounts of by the signs in many ruins we observe today.

There are two main areas in this discussion that will prove that evolutionism is a bogus hypothesis: fossils and radiometric dating. Fossils are typically the imprints of organisms in a sedimentary layer that was compressed and which caused the organism to be crystallized by mineral deposits. There are also fossils of footprints, animal tracks, tail marks, etc. If you think about it, to form a fossil, the burial and compression must be done in a short time, or else the organism simply would rot and would not give enough time for crystallization to take place. With this fact in mind, do you see a big hole starting to develop in uniformitarianism? Even though they may try to convince you, time is not the limiting factor for fossil formation, but the adequate surrounding conditions are. There are fossils that have been found of modern human beings and artifacts dating from the 1800s. It only takes the right conditions to form fossils. Evolutionism wants and needs to suggest long periods of time for our minds to wrap around the concept of evolutionary change.

What Lyell and others after him have done is to arbitrarily date certain layers of sedimentary rocks to fit the long history needed to insinuate the idea that a long period of time occurred in order to accommodate evolution. Then they studied the fossils found in these rocks and used the fossils of extinct organisms found in those layers, called index fossils, to date similar layers in other locations of the globe. This is totally unscientific; in fact, it is based on circular logic and totally contrary to the scientific method of analysis. The fact that no one has had the guts to publicly question this farce shows the total control the so-called "scientific community" has over the information that gets published. The dates on the layers were set arbitrarily back in the 1800s!

You may say, but these dates are confirmed by radiometric dating. Absolutely not! Here is where it sounds like a conspiracy theory (on the "scientific" community's part), but judge it for yourself. Radiometric is the process of decay of a parent material, like uranium 238, into a daughter material, in this case, lead 206. In the process, there is emission of energy in the form of radiation. The time it takes for half the parent material to decay is called the half-life, which for this example, is 4.5 billion years. Measuring the amounts of parent and daughter materials in a sample of rock or soil and knowing the half-life of the process, theoretically, one can determine the age of a sample. Radiometric dating assumes that there is no contamination of parent or daughter material during decay, that there was no daughter material when the sample was formed, and that the decay rate was constant. As you can imagine, none of these assumptions are correct. It is impossible to conceive that a rock will not be contaminated. Water percolates in the soil and rocks, dissolving and leaching minerals and metals to other layers below.

Many used Radiometric dating processes involve lead as the daughter material, and therefore it is usual to find different isotopes of lead in rock or soil samples, which makes determining the Radiometric dating process to date the rock impossible. Also, it is known that radioactive materials capture neutrons from radioactive decay in surrounding rocks; these neutrons change the atomic mass (the number identifying the radioactive material, i.e., uranium 238 versus uranium 235, which lost 3 neutrons), making difficult to determine which Radiometric dating process is to be used. Moreover, intense heat, such as of lava flows or magma extrusions, is known to damage radioactive clocks in rocks and soils.

Using the very few publications that escaped the "scientific" community's censorship provides examples that show Radiometric dating is unreliable, to say the least (note that most of the publications are from the '70s when their grip on the Scientific Society was not so tight). These include: lava flows in Hawaii that occurred in 1800-01 were radio dated between 1.6 and 3 billion years old (Journal Science, 10/11/68); Sunset Crater Volcano lava, dated by tree rings as being about 1,000 years old, was radio dated at 200,000 years old (Journal of Earth & Planetary Science, 6/69); the lava dome in Mount Saint Helen's formed in 1980 was radio dated 2.8 million years old; *living* sea shells gave a carbon 14 date ranging from 440 to 750 years (Mangerud & Gulliksen in Quaternary Research, 1975); *living* trees gave carbon 14 date of 10,000 years (Von Fange, 1974).

It is clear that Radiometric dating, due to the reasons already explained, exaggerates the age of the material it is trying to determine. But this does not deter the "scientists." They do not want to discuss these contradictions, and we keep reading in schoolbooks facts such as these: "the Earth is 3.2 billion years old" or "the Cambrian Period started 540 million years ago and lasted for 40 million years". All bogus information based on 18th century philosophers' pipe dreams (and very likely spiritualist séances) and supported by a "scientific" community that does not have the guts to question it properly just because they cannot conceive the Bible may be right.

The fact is that the only evidence we have of our existence is that humans have been on this Earth for about 6,500 years. From archeological finds, we can tell that humans were never animals, lived in communities, and formed civilizations in different parts of the globe, demonstrating intelligence, craft, and skill comparable to ours (and some greater than ours in some aspects). Different cultures have accounts of a devastating flood (e.g., Babylonians, Mayans, etc.). If we use the ages of the personages provided in the Bible, we can determine that the flood happened approximately 2350 BC. It is conceivable that the Earth before the flood was composed of a single continent (Gondwana) and that this pre-continental drift land did not have tall mountains, hence covering it with water, as is told in the Bible, did not require huge amounts of water. It is also conceivable that during the flood, continental shifts were triggered, as the event is described as hugely catastrophic. The flood must have caused massive amounts of erosion (washing out of the loose dirt off the rising mountain chains at the newly created land masses by collisions of continents), which were then deposited, forming new sedimentary layers, which as the waters receded, have exposed the features such as the Grand Canyon and seashells found in tall mountains.

In this scenario, it is conceivable that the organisms, especially those attached or with limited movement, would have been first to be quickly covered with sediments and subjected to enormous pressure as more sediment kept accumulating over them, forming the fossils on the "older" deeper layers (seashells, snails, trilobites). Also, large numbers of mobile animals huddled on the higher grounds available or next to their source of food, were finally overcome by the waters and also quickly buried by sediments, forming what we find as coal and oil deposits as well as the fossils of more "modern" shallower geologic layers.

These "scientists," especially biologists, forget to apply established principles of physics and thermodynamics to blindly champion evolutionism. It is known that time increases the disorder (or entropy) of things in the universe. Time tends to disperse, not organize things. As a result, one would never expect time to form complex organic molecules from inorganic molecules or for time to form a multicellular organism from unicellular organisms, much less to form a human being from an ape. Organisms within their kind adapt to their environment, but there is no evidence that an organism of one kind has evolved from another kind. Not one fossil of the millions found and studied show that this has ever occurred. Biologists like to mention mutations as the principal mechanism for evolutionism but forget that a very small percentage of all mutations actually have a positive effect on the organism. These negative mutations are lost because the organism either cannot reproduce, or the mutation is corrected when the organism is able to reproduce. The very few positive mutations lead to new versions of proteins that help an organism and its future generations within its kind better adapt to changes in their environment, not to evolve into "higher" beings!

God has created us with a natural homing device. We long to have a relationship with Him, but through the brainwashing, we have been subjected to on an ongoing basis, we have replaced It with other gods. What is It for you? Drugs, sex, gambling, work, power, alcohol, knowledge? Your god is what consumes most of your time… and is killing you! You will never be happy with those gods; they never satisfy. They are never enough. Do you feel there is always something missing even though your life is a relative success? You have everything you need, but you still feel emptiness…, that is the homing device acting upon you. One day, and I hope it will be soon, you will realize that it is time to have a relationship with your creator. The only way to get to God is through His son, who suffered and died for all of your sins. God will not allow you in through your self-righteousness (your actions, as good intentioned as they may be) because you are imperfect. You cannot get into Heaven because you are "good" and do "good things." The only way to get to God is through the righteousness of His son. He can do that because He was perfect. His perfection purchases your sins, but only if you invite Him to be at the helm of your life. The love of God is manifested by the fact that, even though you are imperfect,

He chooses to see you through the perfection of His son. But you need to first invite Him. I pray you will invite Jesus into your life soon. We are talking about the most important thing in your life, your eternal life.

What About Those Who Believe in Buddha?

I respect the Buddhist philosophy because it represents one of the oldest recognitions of the need of spirituality in mankind and its struggle against materialism. It is curious to note some parallels between Jesus and Buddha, such as the temptation by the devil before starting their ministries or the insignificance of an earthly status or gender as a requirement to receive the grace of God. Of course, for you, the grace of God is enlightenment, which is achieved by denying yourself of the world. This is good to a certain degree, as Buddha himself found out. Initially, Buddha began as an ascetic and later realized that this path was not the way to the *truth* but can be, in fact, hurtful if that denial is taken to the extreme.

The Four Noble Truths and the Eightfold Path are the culmination of Buddha's quest for the truth. But this is a culmination of the maximum possible state for an earthly being. It is achieved through incredible personal discipline and dedication. But God created us also to enjoy life. He only asks us to maintain a relationship with Him. Buddhism appears to imply that the only way to have that relationship with God (to know the truth) is to overcome our attachments of material things through wisdom, morality, and meditation. This process is based solely on one's righteousness. Where is God in this process? God requires perfection, and not even Buddha was perfect because he was a man. An extraordinary man, but a man, nonetheless. How do we, which are much less than Buddha, fit in all of this? It is wishful thinking that we will find grace with God by self-righteousness no matter how enlightened we think we are, even if we follow closely Buddha's process.

We are all sinners, no matter how much we deny ourselves the things of this world and how much time we dedicate to meditation. The only way to free ourselves of our sins is through the sacrifice of God himself. For that purpose, He sent his only son Jesus Christ. His blood washes us clean of sin. His righteousness makes us acceptable to God. This must happen first. The denials of this world (sacrifice) and meditation (prayer) would then reinforce your relationship with God. Most Christians are quick to accept Jesus as their Savior and Lord but lack the sacrifice and prayer discipline that you have to maintain the relationship God wants with us. You would be better Christians than most that call themselves Christian. Pray to Jesus to forgive your sins, thank Him for dying for your sins, ask Him to be the Lord in your life, and continue in your current path of pursuing the truth to be assured that your name is written in the Book of Life, which will be open at the end of times. Only those who have their name written will be allowed to remain in the presence of God. "But whoever denies Me before men, him I will also deny before My Father who is in heaven." These are not my words but those of Jesus Himself through Matthew 10:33. No one living person has ever had the authority to say this. I pray that your eyes will be open to this truth.

How Will Things Be Near the End According to The Bible?

One of the aspects in the Bible that make it unique among all other writings about God are its prophecies. No other text has so many descriptions of events to come. This is what makes the Bible credible. Of the 333 references of a Messiah coming found in the Old Testament, 109 have been fulfilled in His first coming. Thus, besides the remaining 224, which will be fulfilled in His second coming, there are many other prophesies of how things will occur towards the end.

One such prophecy is found in Daniel (2:1-49), who was a young boy when he was taken captive by the Babylonians at about 600 BC to serve in Nebuchadnezzar's royal palace. One night during the second year of his reign, the king assembled all his wise men and demanded that they tell him what he had dreamed. As you can imagine, no one could even dare guess. They kept telling the king, "Please tell us the dream, and we will tell you what it means." But the king was obstinate and threatened all of them with doom if they did not comply as requested. They understandably replied: "No one except the gods can tell you your dream, and they do not live here among people." The king then ordered all of his wise men executed. But Daniel interceded and requested more time to reveal the dream, which was allowed by the king. Daniel then prayed to God for mercy by allowing the secret to be known. That night the secret was revealed to Daniel in a vision. The next morning, after praising God in a beautiful thankful prayer, Daniel met the king and revealed the king's secret dream.

The dream was about what was going to happen in the future. It was about a huge, shining, and frightening statue of a man. The head of the statue was made of fine gold, its chest and arms of silver, its belly and thighs of bronze, its legs of iron, and its feet of a combination of iron and baked clay. Then a rock from a mountain, not cut by human hands, struck the feet of iron and clay, smashing them to bits. As a result, the entire statue crumbled into small pieces, and then the wind blew the pieces away without a trace. But the rock that caused the destruction became a great mountain that covered the entire earth. That was what the king had dreamt.

Daniel then proceeded to explain the dream to the king. The head of gold represents you, Nebuchadnezzar, but after your kingdom comes to an end, another kingdom inferior to yours will rise to take your place. After that kingdom has fallen, yet a third kingdom will rise to rule the world. Following that kingdom, there will be a fourth one as strong as iron. What follows this one will be a kingdom divided. While some parts of it will be as strong as iron, other parts will be as weak as clay. These divided kingdoms will try to strengthen by forming intermarriage alliances, but they will not hold together. During the reign of these last kingdoms, God will set up a kingdom that will annihilate them and will never be destroyed or conquered, represented by the rock not cut by human hands smashing the statue and growing until overtaking the entire Earth.

With the advantage of history on our backs, this prophecy can be further explained as this: the head of gold is Nebuchadnezzar's Babylonian kingdom, as told by Daniel. The Babylonian empire territory encompassed today's entire Middle East, the northern Arabic peninsula, eastern Turkey, and Iraq. After Nebuchadnezzar died, his grandson, Belshazzar, became the king of Babylon, but a few years into his kingdom, in 539 BC, Cyrus the Great of Persia conquered Babylon. The Medo-Persians overtook the Babylonian empire and added to its territory today's northern Africa, Bulgaria, the rest of Turkey, Iran, Afghanistan, and parts of Pakistan. The Medo-Persians represent the chest and arms of silver. However, in 334 BC, Alexander the Great of Macedon, in turn, conquered the Medo-Persians, representing the belly and thighs of bronze. They overtook the Medo-Persians and added Egypt and Greece to the territory. The Grecians dominated that entire part of the world until 146 BC, long after Alexander the Great's death in 323 BC. The Roman occupation of the Greek world began after the Battle of Actium on 31 BC, in which Augustus defeated Cleopatra VII, the Greek Ptolemaic queen of Egypt, and the Roman general Mark Antony and a year later conquered Alexandria, the last great city of Hellenistic Greece. The Roman Empire represents the two legs of iron curiously because, in AD 285, the empire was divided in two. The Romans conquered all the kingdoms surrounding the Mediterranean Sea as well as southern Britain. The Roman Empire officially ended in AD 476, but actually it continued to function through several kingdoms, which will be described later. These kingdoms are represented by the feet of iron and clay.

The last book in the Bible written by the only apostle of Jesus still living at the time is the book of Revelation. It was written by John while exiled by the Romans on the island of Patmos in about AD 95. In his vision, John implies that the Roman Empire would eventually change from Pagan beliefs to a politico-religious system. The Pagan form clearly existed since the empire formation in 27 BC until AD 313 when the Emperor Constantine issued the Edict of Milan, which accepted Christianity and, 10 years later, becoming the official religion of the Roman Empire. After successive attacks by hordes of barbarian groups, such as Alaric (from AD 408 to 410), Attila (from AD 442 to 453), and Genseric (from AD 439 to 474), the Roman Empire ended up disappearing for 298 years. However, in the year AD 774, Charlemagne overthrew the kingdom of the Lombards in Northern Italy, receiving the title Patrician of Rome. He reached the height of his power in AD 800 when he was crowned "Emperor of the Romans" by Pope Leo at the Old St. Peter's Basilica in Rome and thus revived the Empire of Rome of the West under its Gothic form. Charlemagne united most of Western Europe for the first time since the classical era of the Roman Empire and even united parts of Europe that had never been under Roman rule. Charlemagne spurred the Carolingian Renaissance, a period of energetic cultural and intellectual activity within the Western Church. This is the rebirth of the Roman Empire under Papal form, also known as the Papacy or Romanism.

Even prior to the death of Charlemagne in AD 814, the Empire was divided among various members of the Carolingian dynasty. These included King Charles the Younger, son of Charlemagne, who received Neustria; King Louis the Pious, who received Aquitaine; and King Pepin, who received Italy. After the death of both Pepin and Charles, the entire Empire passed to Louis, who died in AD 840. The next years were marred by internal strife among the family members that ruled over the various portions of the territory of the Empire.

The Treaty of Verdun in AD 843 finally divided the Empire in three kingdoms: West, Middle, and East Francia. The Treaty triggers a new manner of resolving conflicts and negotiating territory, which created the kingdoms and eventually the countries of Europe we know today. This manner of resolving conflicts took some time to consolidate. However, all these countries are offshoots of the Roman Empire, which continued until its dissolution in 1806 by the Napoleonic Wars. At the end of the Napoleonic Wars in 1815, the only vestiges of the Roman Empire was in the German Confederation.

Yet another book in the Bible provides a different perspective of the prophetic scene. It is the book of Ezekiel. One of his many prophesies involves the reunification of Israel in their original territory in the Middle East, which finally happened in 1948 after 1,878 years of being dispersed throughout the world and suffering several situations of persecution and holocaust. Ezekiel's vision was of dry bones coming together to make a skeleton and being covered with flesh and then coming alive. He then mentions an attack. The traditional *literal* interpretation of Ezekiel's vision (Eze. 38:15-16) is that the source of the aggression involves an invasion of the armies from Russia and Turkey "You will come from your homeland in the distant north with your vast cavalry and your mighty army, and you will attack my people Israel, covering their land like a cloud.." However, the Antichrist destroys the invading forces, apparently using atomic weapons. "I will send torrential rain, hailstones, fire, and burning sulfur!" (Eze. 38:22). "After seven months, teams of men will be appointed to search the land for skeletons to bury, so the land will be made clean again. Whenever bones are found, a marker will be set up so the burial crews will take them to be buried." (Eze. 39:14-15). Possibly a description of land decontamination by removal of bodies after radioactive fallout.

Now that the Antichrist is admired and trusted by the Jewish people, he sets up a statue of himself in the newly built Temple on the Temple Mount that he brokered a few year prior this conflict and demands to be worshiped. This is called by Daniel the "Abomination of Desolation," which was also referred to by Jesus when he described the end times. It is then that the Jewish people realize that their leader and protector is not of God. They rebel, and a new Jewish persecution period begins.

This marks the second half of what is known as the Great Tribulation Period. Everyone is forced to accept a mark on the forehead or hand to indicate allegiance with the Antichrist. A lot of speculation surrounds this mark. Some think it will be a branding, others a below the skin microchip, which would contain each person's identification. We currently have the technology to do this, as we do to identify pets. No one will be allowed to work, shop, travel, etc., without the mark. Those who reject the mark and the Antichrist are put to death. Many believe that this mid Tribulation time is when Satan is cast from heaven to Earth because literally "hell breaks loose" on Earth after this time.

The Word of God, the Bible, needs to be read literally and in context, except when it obviously is telling us something in images, parables, or in visions. These images, parables, and visions, in most cases, are even followed by an actual explanation in the Bible. The book of Revelation is for the most part one exception, as only a few symbolic messages are explained. But God says in Revelation 1:3: "God blesses the one who reads the words of this prophecy to the church, and he blesses all who listen to its message and obey what it says, for the time is near." In other words, God wants us to read and understand His revelation of the future, but requires us to put some effort to grasp its meanings. God has given us many symbolic interpretations throughout the Bible, such as Nebuchadnezzar's dream of the giant statue made up of different materials, among many others. We should use all these interpretations to understand Revelation.

In symbology, an object is chosen to represent not itself but something of analogous character. Every symbol, regardless of the department from which it is taken, whether from the material universe, the animal kingdom, human life, or the heavenly realm, stands as the representative, not of itself, but of some other object of analogous character not found in the same department from which it is drawn. From this introduction, and using deduction and logic, we can introduce a set of rules for the interpretation of symbols. Some of these rules are summarized in the following table with an example right below it:

Symbol	Analogous Meaning
Elements drawn from nature/animal world	Political events of the empire
Example: A wild, ferocious beast, stamping upon or devouring everything within its reach	A cruel, persecuting, tyrannical government. Anti-Christian persecuting power of Rome
Elements drawn from human and angelic life	Religious or spiritual events of the church
Example: An angel from heaven, with his face as the sun, his feet as pillars of fire, and a rainbow upon his head	The glorious body of God's reformers
Elements drawn from the Old Testament	Affairs of the church

Symbol	Analogous Meaning
Example: A candlestick or lampstand	A church
A combination of symbols drawn from the departments of human life and animal life	Politico-religious system
Example: A woman and a beast	The civil powers of Europe and the ecclesiastical power of Rome
A living, active, intelligent agent, its actions, and the effects of its actions	An analogous intelligent agent, its actions, and the effects of its actions
Example: A fallen star	The propagator of a false faith
Time	Days as in years
Example: Five months	5 * 30 days/month = 150 years
Example: An hour, and a day, and a month, and a year	(1/24)*360 + 1 + 30 + 360 days/year = 391 years and 15 days
Example: For a time, times, and half a time	1 + 2 + ½ = 3.5 * 360 days/year = 1,260 years

When people read the book of Revelation (Apocalypse in Greek), they tend to read it in today's terms. That is, as if every vision is about something that is to come in *our* future. That is not completely so. The great majority of the visions are about events that have already occurred. They were definitely present and future events for John the Apostle back in AD 95. The proof of this is the fact that the timeline provided in the visions coincide with what happened in history, both on the political and religious aspects, between AD 95 and today. John is ordered (Rev. 1:19) to "write down what you have seen, both the things that are *now* happening and the things that *will* happen." The visions, which are described in apparent complicated symbology, summarize events that occurred in our history, then flashes back into scenes in heaven, much like a good movie. This causes a lot of confusion and has frustrated many faithful readers of the Word of God.

The Revelation Explained by F. G. Smith (1918), who methodically goes through the different manners of symbolism used in the last book of the Bible by John the Apostle, was used here to summarize what the book of Revelation attempts to convey. God gave John a vision to write and prove to us that His story is true, just as He has done with all the previous prophets who wrote their visions of what was to come. However, God closes His story with this amazing account of the future history of the known world, centered, as it is throughout the entire Bible (Old and New Testament), on Jesus and His church. The timeline of the vision is from John's time (about AD 95) to the end of the world. We have today the particular advantage of 1,925 years of history for a more complete understanding of the vision's meaning.

Most who read the book of Revelation, including certain pastors of congregations, who are used to reading and expounding the Bible literally, become confused by its symbology, which cannot be understood literally. In fact, in many passages of the book, the text itself explains some of the symbology so as to not lead people astray. In those cases, I have bolded the explanation on the "What it means" column. The visions follow the historical chronology, but sometimes changes scenes and repeats some events but from a different perspective. God orders John (Rev. 22:10), "Do not seal up the prophetic words in this book, for the time is near." From this, we can interpret that the true Church of God should read and understand the book of Revelation as intended to be understood. I hope that the analysis presented here, which can probably be improved upon, will clarify things and place the book in its rightful perspective. The analysis will begin with Chapter IV because this is when the vision of end times begins.

Chapter IV

What it says	What it means
Introduction to the throne of God	A great monarch in a position of authority
The 24 elders in white robes	Ministers of God representing Old and New Testament
The seven lamps*	The seven Spirits of God
The four living creatures	The redeemed from four corners of the Earth
-covered in eyes	-vigilance and superior discernment
-one like a lion	-strength and courage
-one like an ox	-sacrifice or of patient labor
-one like a man	-reason and intelligence
-one like an eagle	-swiftness and far-sighted vision

*Seven represents completeness and perfection. It is repeatedly used as part of the symbology.

God in its infinite greatness and power is on His heavenly throne surrounded by His ministers, the redeemed by Jesus and the Holy Spirit.

Chapter V

What it says	What it means
God holds a scroll	The infinite counsels and purposes of God
-written on both sides	-those purposes are full and complete
-with seven seals	-the contents were unrevealed until then
-held on His right hand	-able to carry into execution His purposes
A slaughtered Lamb	Jesus after His sacrifice at Calvary
-with seven horns	-having fulness of power
-and seven eyes	**-having the seven spirits of God**
The Lamb takes the scroll from God	The plan of redemption is revealed
The 24 elders had harps & vials full of incense	**The prayers of the redeemed**

God hands Jesus, the only one able to carry on His will for the Earth concerning His church, and His plan of redemption, while the redeemed multitude sing and pray.

Chapter VI

What it says	What it means
Jesus opens the first seal	
A rider on a white horse	Humble minister of Jesus
-with a bow	-having strength and power
-and a crown	-wearing a victor's crown
-to conquer	-to spread the Word of God
Jesus opens the second seal	
A rider on a red horse	Agent of great destruction
-power to make war	-propagator of the Pagan religions
-with a great sword	-able and willing to destroy
Jesus opens the third seal	Dark or appalling in its nature
A rider on a black horse	Brings great apostasy and spiritual darkness
-with a pair of scales	-severe exactions upon the people
Jesus opens the fourth seal	
A rider on a pale horse named Death	Agent of ghastly, terrible nature
-followed by Hell	-causing persecutions of the Papacy
-authority to kill, famine, disease, etc.	-every means of cruelty imaginable is used to exterminate "heresy"
Jesus opens the fifth seal	
All that were martyred for the Word of God are under the altar wearing white robes and ask to be avenged but are told to wait	After Pagan Rome came the apostate church of Rome (Papacy), but the period of tribulation of the true church is not yet over

What it says	What it means
Jesus opens the sixth seal	
-a great earthquake	-military incursions cause political changes
-the sun darkens	-kings and princes being removed
-the moon is red	-overthrow of dignitaries in the empire
-the stars fall from the sky	-the entire ruling class is affected
-mountains and islands are moved	-the entire fabric of civil government changes
-everyone hides in caves	-terror of the population

This is a summary introduction to what will come. The early Christian church is persecuted and martyred by Pagan Roman religion, bringing spiritual darkness. Paganism is then replaced by the Papacy, and soon after, tribulations of the true church continue, now at the hands of the Papacy. Barbarian hordes repeatedly attack the Roman Empire, bringing terror and destruction. Roman society is in a state of agitation, kingdoms are overthrown, and their rulers and princes removed from their positions of power or made objects of the most gloomy terror. The population flees in total horror and panic.

Chapter VII

What it says	What it means
Four angels at the four corners of Earth -holding the four winds	The hordes of barbarians, under their leaders -precipitating themselves from all sides
Another angel coming from the east orders not to harm the earth until servants are sealed	God keeps them under restraint until the church is established throughout the empire
-sealing of the 144,000	-God's church, comprising the true Israel
-12,000 from each tribe of Israel	-perfect and complete, no part being omitted
Multitude in white robes A vast crowd, too great to count, from every nation and tribe and people and language, standing in front of the throne and before the Lamb. They have washed their robes in the blood of the Lamb and made them white	**The ones who died in the great tribulation** The scene is laid in heaven and refers undoubtedly to the end of time and the final glorious triumph of all who endure unto the end

At this point, the story rewinds a bit to tell us that the barbarians were actually held under restraint by God to ensure that the church was well-established in the empire before they begin their attacks. There is a flashback to the heavenly scene that shows those who were martyred by Rome Pagan, Rome Papal, Protestantism, and by the final persecutions carried over by the antichrist.

Chapter VIII

What it says	What it means
Jesus breaks the seventh seal	
-silence for half an hour	-literal silence before the beginning of the end
-seven angels with seven trumpets	-total civil and ecclesiastical persecuting powers
-angel with gold incense burner	-the trials and triumphs of the true church
The incense burner with fire is thrown to Earth with much noise, and an earthquake	The revolutions and convulsions now about to take place in the empire
The first angel sounds trumpet	
-hail and fire mixed with blood	-Alaric vandals attacking Romans
-one-third of the Earth set on fire	-calamity from outside of the empire
-one-third of trees burned	-those not able to resist and defend themselves
-all the grass burned	-feebler portion of society suffered the most
The second angel sounds trumpet	
-a great mountain of fire thrown into the sea	-permanent instrument of destruction at the heart of the empire with bloody consequences
-one third of the sea became blood	-Genseric repetitive attacks from Africa to the Mediterranean coasts of the empire

What it says	What it means
-one-third of the living things at sea died	-the power of the ruling class is diminished
-one-third of the ships at sea destroyed	-peace and commerce is compromised
The third angel sounds trumpet	
-a great star fell from the sky	-appear suddenly and soon disappear with bitter results
-fell on one-third of the rivers	-Attila attacks the heart of Europe
-fell on the springs of water	-then focuses on the periphery of the empire, dying suddenly
-one-third of the water made bitter	-leaving bitter results to the empire
-many people died from that bitter water	-literal
The fourth angel sounds trumpet	
-one-third of the sun was struck	-loss of kings and princes
-one-third of the moon became dark	-loss of dignitaries in the empire
-one-third of the stars became dark	-loss of the ruling class
Angel flying yelling woe, woe, woe	Announces that the three trumpets yet to sound will possess greater calamities to the people of Rome than those who have preceded

There is a suspensive silence before Jesus begins to develop what will happen next. It details the intensive, frequent, violent, and disastrous attacks to the Roman Empire by three main groups of barbarian hordes: Alaric, Genseric, and Attila. For three centuries, Rome Pagan slaughtered millions of the Lord's innocent Christian servants. The hand of retributive Justice was finally extended to humble Rome through the barbaric hordes. However, more is to come.

Chapter IX

What it says	What it means
The fifth angel sounds trumpet	
-a star falls and is given the key to the pit	-civil and religious propagator of a false faith
-smoke comes out of the pit	-delusive faith proceeding from the dark
-darkens the sun	-obscuring the truth
-of the smoke come out locusts	-Islamic Saracens
-ordered to not hurt the trees or the grass	-not sent as a scourge upon the political but to set forth an awful religious imposture
-to hurt only those who do not have the seal of God to be tormented for five months	-to anguish the Roman Empire for one hundred and fifty years (612-762 AD)
-men seeking death will not find it	-no one would be able to avoid them
-locust-like battle horses	-multitude well-armed
-with crowns like gold and faces of men	-great success and triumphs and boldness
-hair like women, teeth like lions	-effeminateness and ferocity of character

What it says	What it means
-breastplates of iron	-insensibility to injuries
-sound of wings like many horses running	-multitude and rapidity of their conquests
-tails like scorpions	-propagators of a false faith
-their king was the angel of the pit	-demonic in origin
The sixth angel sounds trumpet Release of the four angels that were bound at the great Euphrates River	Four Sultanies of the Ottoman Empire with their capital Bagdad wait for the allotted time
-to kill one-third of the population	-attacking from outside the Roman Empire
-200 million mounted troops	-vast army
-armor was fiery red, dark blue, and yellow	-character of the Turks as a religious system
-horses had heads like lions	-invincible strength and courage
-fire and smoke billowed from their mouths	-Moslems as a political power
-power was in their mouths and in their tails	-a political and military power
But the people who did not die in these plagues still refused to repent of their evil deeds and turn to God. And they did not repent of their murders or their witchcraft or their sexual immorality or their thefts	The Papacy had reached the summit of apostasy and iniquity, the virgin Mary, the saints, and thousands of idols in the form of miserable relics being worshiped more than God

The attacks continue, but now they are not only military but religious as well. The Islamic Saracens bring with them a false faith that harasses and further debilitates the Roman Empire for a period of 150 years. This is followed, a time later, by the attacks of the Moslem Ottoman Empire, possessing enormous political and military power. These attacks are hinted to be the result of the apostasy of the Papacy.

Chapter X

What it says	What it means
Angel with a small scroll	
-holding a scroll that was open	-God's revealed will
-right foot on the sea and left foot on the land	-promulging the message among all nations
-swore an oath in the name of God	-proclaiming the will of God
-great shout like the roar of a lion	-with strength and courage
-seven thunders answered	-voice of God?
-John is ordered not to document the answer	-literal
John takes the scroll and eats it	The church receiving the Word from ministers
-sweet in the mouth, sour in the stomach	-the eagerness with which people receive the Word of God and the bitter persecutions and oppositions that results

There is a pause to the main story with a few flashbacks into the heavenly scene. A special messenger appearing on earth with the awful message that the end of time will be after the seventh angel sounds its trumpet. The message of the pure gospel is to be preached not only in the Roman Empire but throughout the world. Also that the gospel will be received with eagerness but will be followed by opposition and persecution.

Chapter XI

What it says	What it means
Measuring the temple of God -count the number of worshipers	-visible Church of God with its doctrines
-do not measure the outer courtyard	-it constitutes the church of Rome
-trampling the holy city for 42 months	-given to the Gentiles to profane 1,260 years
-power to the two witnesses clothed in burlap	-Word and Spirit of God in the church
-they will prophesy for 1,260 days	-profane church ruled from AD 270 to 1530
-anyone who tries to harm them must die	-no one could challenge their power
-power to turn the rivers and oceans into blood	-power to excommunicate and interdict
-strike the Earth with every kind of plague	-became the terror of individuals and the scourge of nations
Death & resurrection of the witnesses	

What it says	What it means
-the beast from the bottomless pit declares war against the two witnesses and kills them	-Protestantism ends up opposing the Word and Spirit of God. The Bible no longer is considered the Word of God to them
-everyone will stare at their bodies for three and a half days	- 350 years of Protestantism to finally recognize that Word and Spirit are the sole Governors of the true church
-God breathed life into the two witnesses, and they stood up!	-since 1880, God began to raise up holy men and women to preach the unadulterated gospel
-a loud voice from heaven called to the two witnesses, "Come up here!"	-at the allotted time, God will snatch up or rapture His church from earth
-at the same time, a terrible earthquake destroys a tenth of the city, and 7,000 die	-future political upheaval as the countries and empires are all overthrown
The seventh angel sounds trumpet	
-loud voices shouting in heaven proclaiming the Kingdom of Christ	-angels announcing that Jesus is now taking over possession of the earth
-the 24 elders worship God and declare that the time of God's wrath has come	-the redeemed in heaven declaring that the time of God has finally arrived
-the Temple of God is opened, and the Ark of His covenant could be seen inside the Temple	-demonstrating that the old and new covenants are part and parcel of God's plan
-lightning, thunder, an earthquake, and a terrible hailstorm	-great commotion and destruction that will not take much time

Still in the heavenly scene, we are told that the Papacy will be ruled by non-Christians for 1,260 years and that the Word and Spirit of God will be driven into obscurity by Protestantism given their power to excommunicate and interdict true Christians. But after the allotted time, the Word and Spirit of God will again be preached through the unadulterated gospel. After this, the true church will be raptured to heaven, thus initiating the end. At that time, Jesus will claim back the Earth.

Chapter XII

What it says	What it means
The woman clothed with the sun	The Church of God under the new covenant
-the moon beneath her feet	-symbol of the old covenant
-a crown of twelve stars on her head	-the twelve apostles of the Lamb
-pregnant and in labor pains	-tribulations that the church is to suffer
-the son was to rule all nations with iron rod	-the Truth will prevail
Large red dragon	A tyrannical, persecuting government
-seven heads	-the seven forms of Roman government
-and ten horns	-the ten minor kingdoms
-with seven crowns on his heads	-seven kingdoms with supreme authority and power
-swept away one-third of the stars and threw them to the Earth	-Pagan Rome engaging in persecution, torture, and death against the ministers of the Church of God and its followers

What it says	What it means
-ready to devour the woman's baby	-new converts can find the same end
-baby snatched away from the dragon to God	-God provides strength to endure
-the woman fled into the wilderness	-the church disperses and hides
-protected by God for 1,260 days	- protected by God for 1,260 years.
- war in heaven between Michael and his angels and the dragon (Satan) and his angels	- the Devil suffered a severe defeat when the Pagan Roman Empire realized that Christianity could not be destroyed, and the pagans were cast down from their lofty positions
- the dragon lost and was thrown down to the Earth with all his angels	
- They have defeated him by the blood of the Lamb and by their testimony	- literal
- the dragon pursues the woman who had given birth to the male child	- Rome Pagan continues to harass the Church
-she was given two wings to escape to a place prepared for her in the wilderness	- God's grace and providence protects the Church from her enemies
- she would be protected for time, times, and half a time	- protected by God for 1,260 years.
- the dragon tried to drown the woman with a flood of water that flowed from his mouth	- Rome Pagan's last-ditch effort to destroy Christianity through Diocletian (AD 302-312)

What it says	What it means
- the Earth helped her by opening its mouth and swallowing the river - the dragon was angry at the woman and declared war against the rest of her children - then the dragon took his stand on the shore besides the sea	- Constantine (AD 313) issues an edict of toleration in favor of Christians - Rome Pagan determines to make war upon the individual members of the Church - Rome Pagan's influence continues blended between the political and religious

Here we have a recap of the already told story in a summary format. The Old Testament and the New Testament are part and parcel of the entire story. The true church that Jesus left after His sacrifice and resurrection will go through tribulations, but at the end, truth will prevail. However, before this happens, we are reminded that the church will endure persecutions and tribulations for a very long time.

Chapter XIII

What it says	What it means
Beast rising up out of the sea -seven heads and ten horns	-the Roman empire changing from its seven forms of government to ten minor kingdoms
-ten crowns in its horns	-ten kingdoms with supreme authority and power
-names written that blasphemed God	-Rome Papal
-looked like a leopard	-same beast clothed in Christian garb

What it says	What it means
-the dragon gave it great authority	-a tyrannical, persecuting government
The beast	
-one of the heads wounded	-the reformation wounded the Papacy
-fatal wound was healed	-Papacy almost disappeared in 1806 & 1848
-everyone marveled at this miracle	-the formation of the Vatican State (1929) saved the Papacy
-allegiance to the beast	-human organization (religion) is assumed
-worshiped the dragon	-believing in a religious system
-speaks great blasphemies against God	-adopting rites and ceremonies purely Pagan
-was given authority for 42 months	-active for 1,260 years
-allowed to wage war against God's people	-persecuted, tortured, killed the true Christians
-everyone who's name was not written in the Book of Life worshiped the beast	-ecclesiastical power
The beast as a lamb	
-came up out of the earth	-the territory of the Roman empire
-had two horns	-England and Germany (Protestantism)
-spoke with the voice of a dragon	-imitation of the Papal original
-required all the earth to worship the beast	-ecclesiastical power over the entire empire

What it says	What it means
-whose fatal wound had been healed	-Papacy almost disappeared in 1806 & 1848
-did astounding miracles	-the formation of the Vatican State (1929) saved the Papacy
-ordered a great statue of the first beast	-possessed the characteristics of the Papacy
-permitted to give life to this statue	-ecclesiastical powers of Protestantism
-commanded that everyone had to worship it	-authoritative rules of faith and manners
-anyone refusing to worship must die	-must adopt the religion or be persecuted
-required everyone to be given a mark on the right hand or forehead	-Vicarius Filii Dei or Vicar of the Son of God is the Pope's inscription, whose letters add up to 666
-receive the "number of his name" (666)	**-the number representing his name**

The recap continues with the transformation of the Roman Empire from its Pagan state to the Papacy (although it was merely a change of garb). The Reformation provided a heavy blow to the Papacy, but the Protestant movement ended up assuming a similar religious system than the Catholics, with similar disastrous outcome for the true Christians. It predicts that the Papacy would almost disappear but would eventually be saved. The "mark of the beast" is represented by the title assumed by the Pope, which is actually the belief on a religion when God requires instead the simple belief of the Word and Spirit.

Chapter XIV

What it says	What it means
The lamb and the 144,000	
-144,000 on Mount Zion	-perfect and complete Church of God
-144,000 had God's name written on forehead	-the true people of God are with the Lamb
-choir sang a wonderful new song in heaven	-the redeemed people praise God
-angel carrying the Good News to Earth	-the restoration of gospel truth (since 1880)
-angel shouting "Babylon is fallen"	-Protestantism is morally and spiritually fallen
-angel warning anyone taking the mark	-reject religion
The son of man likeness on a white cloud	
-had a gold crown on his head	-entity of God with authority
-a sharp sickle in his hand	-to harvest the Church of God
-angel from Temple tells to swing the sickle	-the work of the reformation taking place
-angel from Temple with sickle	-entity of God with a task
-angel from altar to destroy with fire	-to cut off the wicked
-blood from the winepress	-the final destruction of the wicked

Still in the heavenly scene, there is a reaffirmation that the true church is with Jesus and that the belief in a religion does not save. A sense of urgency is revealed by the fact that the harvest of God is near.

Chapter XV

What it says	What it means
The seven angels holding seven plagues -the people victorious over the beast and statue	-the true Church of God
-holding harps and singing the song of Moses	-song of redemption and song of deliverance
-seven angels come out of the Temple	-complete and divine judgment
-each angel is given a gold bowl	-each judgment with a different effect
-each bowl filled with the wrath of God	-by the divine command as ministers of vengeance

This is a prologue to a new set of events that will continue to affect the European territory, as the story is only interested in following the events surrounding the church.

Chapter XVI

What it says	What it means
First angel with bowl -poured out his bowl on the Earth	-affects the territory of the ten kingdoms
-horrible, malignant sores broke out	-the corruption of all morals
Second angel with bowl	French Revolution (1789)
-poured on the sea	-affects the inhabitants of the ten kingdoms

What it says	What it means
-became like the blood of a corpse	-slaughter and massacre of the inhabitants
-everything in the sea died	-destruction of the kings, rulers, and princes
Third angel with bowl	France's open hostility toward monarchies
-poured out his bowl on the rivers and springs	-affects the monarchies surrounding France
-they became blood	-Europe's insurrections and desolating wars
Fourth angel with bowl	Military empire of Napoleon
-poured out his bowl on the sun	-affects the tyrant ruler
-scorch everyone with its fire	-military campaigns and bloody battles
-they cursed God and did not repent	-France rejects God
Fifth angel with bowl	
-poured out his bowl on the beast's throne	-affects the Holy Roman Empire
-his kingdom was plunged into darkness	-downfall of the Papacy in 1806 and 1848
Sixth angel with bowl	
-poured out his bowl on the great Euphrates	-affects the area of the Euphrates River
-it dried up so that the kings from the east could march their armies toward the west without hindrance	-bringing knowledge and understanding on how to defeat the Holy Roman Empire without impediments

What it says	What it means
-three evil spirits that looked like frogs leaping from the mouths of the dragon, the beast, and the false prophet	-Paganism (mouth of the dragon), Romanism (mouth of the beast), and Protestantism (mouth of the false prophet), spirits of devils
-gather the rulers of the world for battle against the Lord at Armageddon	-to form a confederation and to array themselves against the cause of Christ
Seventh angel with bowl	
-poured out his bowl into the air	-affects the entire world
-God says, "It is finished!"	-the complete and final overthrow of all the great powers; civil and ecclesiastical
-thunder crashed and rolled	-wondrous commotions
-lightning flashed	-will happen suddenly
-a great earthquake struck	-sudden convulsions
-Babylon split into three sections	-heathenism, Catholicism, and Protestantism
-the cities of many nations fell into rubble	-wide destruction of the political apparatus
-every island disappeared and all the mountains were leveled	-the fabric of civil government disappears
-terrible hailstorm with huge hailstones	-fierce but temporary attacks

It begins with pointing out the moral breakdown of the ruling class, which set the scene for the French Revolution and the slaughter and massacre of the monarchy. This, in turn, broke the moral principles of the people to such a level that they ended up rejecting God, triggering soon after the "reign of terror." Soon after, Napoleon enters the scene and wages war on Europe with numerous bloody wars, ending the Papacy. The story is interrupted with a digression to resume the historical events and setting the stage for the final events. It ends with the final overthrow of all the great powers, civil and ecclesiastical, associated with what will occur at the end of the world.

Chapter XVII

What it says	What it means
Angel shows the judgment	
-the great prostitute	-the church of Rome
-rules over many waters	-her wide supremacy in the world over distant peoples and nations
-kings have committed adultery with her	-willing partakers in the church's abominable idolatries
-people drunk by the wine of her immorality	-people blinded by rituals and traditions
-woman sitting on a scarlet beast, had seven heads and ten horns	**-the great city that rules over the kings of the world** that was the Roman Empire
-blasphemies against God were written	-the Pope's title "Vicar of the Son of God"

What it says	What it means
-purple and scarlet clothing and jewelry	-the close relationship that the church had with the civil powers
-she held a gold goblet full of obscenities	-blasphemous assumptions of the Papacy
-"Babylon the Great, Mother of All Prostitutes and Obscenities in the World"	-the center of the earth's idolatry system
-drunk with the blood of God's holy people	**-the witnesses for Jesus**
Angel Explains	
The beast was once alive but isn't now, and yet he will soon come up out of the bottomless pit and go to eternal destruction. The people who belong to this world will be amazed at the reappearance of this beast who had died.	**Five kings have already fallen, the sixth now reigns, and the seventh is yet to come, but his reign will be brief.** Roman Kings, Dictators, Decemvirate, Tribunes, and Triumvirate have already occurred. Currently (for John) under Imperial and in the future, Papal
-the seven heads of the beast	**-seven hills where the woman rules,** seven forms of government under which the Roman empire subsisted
-the scarlet beast that was, but is no longer	**-is the eighth king like the seventh** (Holy Roman Empire after the brief Papal pause)

What it says	What it means
-the ten horns of the beast	**-ten kings who have not yet risen to power. They will be appointed to their kingdoms for one brief moment to reign with the beast**
-will all agree to give the beast their power and authority	-the kings will support and uphold the Papacy
-together, they will go to war against the Lamb	-kings and clergy will persecute the true church
-the Lamb will defeat them	-the true church will overcome
-the waters where the prostitute is ruling	**-people of every nation and language**

Here again, it describes the characteristics of the blasphemous Papal church and an explanation of how the Roman Empire disappears for a while and then reappears as the Holy Roman Empire.

Chapter XVIII

What it says	What it means
Another angel announces -"Babylon is fallen, that great city is fallen!"	-fall of heathenism, Catholicism, Protestantism
-has become a home for demons	-her moral fall is the grand signal for the escape of God's people
for all the nations have fallen because of the wine of her passionate immorality	

What it says	What it means
-the kings of the world have committed adultery with her **Warning that God remembers her evil deeds**	-political powers support the apostate religions God's word of truth will brings to light all the wickedness and abominations
God's judgment comes in an instant -the merchants of the world weep and mourn, and they watch the smoke ascend	-"the Lord shall consume with the spirit of his mouth and shall destroy with the brightness of his coming."
A mighty angel picked up a huge boulder and threw it into the ocean -the great Babylon will be thrown similarly	Idolatry in eternal doom is pictured and remains to be yet fulfilled -religions in eternal doom

The story continues stating that blasphemy persists with the apostate religions of the world, which is why God will first demonstrate their wickedness and abominations, followed by a complete destruction.

Chapter XIX

What it says	What it means
Vast crowd praising the Lord	Praise came from the lips of the angelic crowd
-the wedding feast of the Lamb	-to celebrate the union of Jesus and His church
-his bride has prepared herself	-the church has resisted the beast
-given to wear the finest of pure white linen	**-the good deeds of God's holy people**
-blessed are those who are invited	-there is much rejoicing in heaven
Heaven opened, a white horse was standing	Glorious conquest at Jesus second advent
-its rider was named Faithful and True	-Jesus in his infinite dignity and majesty
-on his head were many crowns	-his supreme dominion
-his eyes were like flames of fire	-the work of vengeance upon His enemies
-wore a robe dipped in blood	-the blood of His enemies
-his title was the Word of God	-literal
-followed by the armies of heaven, dressed in the finest of pure white linen, on white horses	-the "ten thousands of His saints" manifesting their purity of spirit

What it says	What it means
-from his mouth came a sharp sword	-the Word of God
-will rule the nations with an iron rod	-sin is not tolerated
An angel standing in the sun	
-vultures flying high in the sky	-unattainable power
-"Come and eat the flesh of kings"	-the final and eternal destruction of the allied powers of sin
-the beast and the kings of the world and their armies come to fight against Jesus	-the apostate church and the leaders of the world face Jesus
-the beast and the prophet were captured	-Catholicism and Protestantism are destroyed
-thrown alive into the fiery lake of fire	-their believers are sent to Hell
-their entire army was killed by the sharp sword	-the Word of God destroys apostasy and idolatry
-the vultures gorged themselves on the bodies	-the final destruction of the apostate church

This is about things to happen in the future, most probably after the rapture of the true church. Jesus, followed by a host of His saints, completely destroys the false church and the political leaders of the world by the double-edged sword of His word and sends them to Hell.

Chapter XX

What it says	What it means
Angel with the key to the bottomless pit	
-heavy chain in his hand	-the power to bind
-seized the dragon	-held the public deceiver of the nations
-bound him in chains for a thousand years	-isolated for an indefinite length of time
-threw him into the bottomless pit	-was sent to hell
-Satan could not deceive the nations anymore	-evil would no longer have power
-After a thousand years, he must be released for a little while	-literal?
Judgment	
-people in thrones given the authority to judge	-exalted privilege which Christ promised
-the souls of those who had been beheaded	-spirits of those martyred will be reigning with Christ in Paradise
-reign with Christ for a thousand years	-will reign with Christ forever
-the second death holds no power, they will be priests of God and of Christ and will reign with Him a thousand years	-only those who had part in the first resurrection, the second death will have no power and will live in God's presence forever

What it says	What it means
After the thousand years	
-Satan will be let out of his prison	-literal
-he will go out to deceive Gog and Magog	-literal
-he will gather them together for battle	-a fierce battle between truth and error
-surround God's people and the beloved city	-literal
-fire from heaven consumed them	-literal
-the devil is thrown into the fiery lake of fire	-Satan is sent to Hell
-they will be tormented day and night forever	-literal
Great white throne judgment	
-the earth and sky fled from his presence	-literal dissolution of this world when Christ comes
-they found no place to hide	-literal
-the dead, great and small, before God	-the actions of men are perfectly known and remembered as if they had been recorded in the archives of heaven
-the books were opened	-literal
-all judged according to what they had done	-literal

What it says	What it means
-the sea gave up its dead	-literal
-the grave and Hell gave up their dead, this is the second death	-people of Hell are also judged
-anyone whose name was not recorded in the Book of Life was thrown into the lake of fire	-those who did not accept Jesus as their Lord and Savior

The story continues with more details after the defeat of the false church and corrupt political leaders. Satan is cast into hell forever. The true church will live with Jesus in heaven. God dissolves the world.

Chapter XXI

What it says	What it means
A new heaven and a new Earth -the new Jerusalem, from God out of heaven. "Look, God's home is now among his people!" He will wipe every tear from their eyes; there will be no more death or sorrow or crying or pain -"Look, I am making everything new!"	-"The day of the Lord will come as a thief in the night; in which the heavens shall pass away with a great noise, and the elements shall melt with fervent heat, the Earth also and the works that are therein shall be burned up" -literal

What it says	What it means
-"It is finished! I am the Alpha and the Omega, the Beginning and the End. To all who are thirsty, I will give freely from the springs of the water of life. All who are victorious will inherit all these blessings, and I will be their God, and they will be my children. But cowards, unbelievers, the corrupt, murderers, the immoral, those who practice witchcraft, idol worshipers, and all liars, their fate is in the fiery lake of burning sulfur. This is the second death."	-God announces the fact that He has now fulfilled all that He designed from the beginning
An angel shows John the Holy City	
-Jerusalem, descending out of heaven from God	-the home of the redeemed
-it shone with the glory of God and sparkled like a precious stone. Angel measures the city, its gates, and its wall. Its length and width, and height were each 1,400 miles; the walls were 216 feet thick	-heaven will be a place of wondrous beauty and transcendent glory, as shown by the fact that everything which is considered grand and glorious on Earth is here chosen to describe the home of the redeemed

What it says	What it means
-the wall was made of jasper, and the city was made of pure gold. The twelve gates were made of pearls	-the symbols selected to describe heaven are objects of such priceless worth, even exceeding royal splendor, that we pause in astonishment
-God Almighty and the Lamb are its temple	-literal
-the glory of God illuminates the city and the Lamb is its light	-God is light
-there is no night there	-God is eternal
-nothing evil will be allowed to enter	-the walls represent the security of Zion, whose inhabitants within it can rest in peace and safety

This part and the next gives us a glimpse of how things would be in heaven, description that has no words to do it justice.

Chapter XXII

What it says	What it means
An angel shows John a river with the Water of Life	
-clear as crystal	-purity extreme
-flowing from the throne of God and of the Lamb	-God and Jesus are the source of the "water of life"
-on each side of the river grew a tree of life	-man's heavenly immortality or incorruption
-bearing twelve crops of fruit, with a fresh crop each month	-it blooms and bears fruit abundantly, continuously

What it says	What it means
-the leaves were used for medicine to heal the nations -God's name will be written on their foreheads -"Everything you have heard and seen is trustworthy and true. The Lord God, who inspires his prophets, has sent his angel to tell his servants what will happen soon. Look, I am coming soon! Blessed are those who obey the words of prophecy written in this book." -when John heard and saw this, he fell down to worship at the feet of the angel -but the angel said: "Worship only God!" -then the angel added: "Do not seal up the prophetic words in this book, for the time is near. Let the one who is doing harm continue to do harm; let the one who is vile continue to be vile; let the one who is righteous continue to live righteously; let the one who is holy continue to be holy.	-the privilege is open to all God's people The language of symbols stops here

What it says	What it means
Look, I am coming soon, bringing my reward with me to repay all people according to their deeds. I am the Alpha and the Omega, the First and the Last, the Beginning and the End." -"Blessed are those who wash their robes. They will be permitted to enter through the gates of the city and eat the fruit from the tree of life. Outside the city are the dogs, the sorcerers, the sexually immoral, the murderers, the idol worshipers, and all who love to live a lie." -Jesus himself added: "If anyone adds anything to what is written here, God will add to that person the plagues described in this book. And if anyone removes any of the words from this book of prophecy, God will remove that person's share in the tree of life and in the holy city that are described in this book."	

Summary

The events outlined of what prophetically did happen (from the 1st to the 21st century) and what is going to happen on earth in the future are amazing. It appears to describe to the letter and within a specific timeline our political and religious history. As already pointed out, not the entire earth's history, only the political and ecclesiastical history surrounding God's church. The predicted events that occurred recently (the re-establishment of the State of Israel) and the precursing events that are currently happening (Turkey breaking its historical alliance with Israel and becoming close to Russia) should dissipate in us any doubts about what will occur in the future.

It begins with a wonderful vision of God's throne and His court composed of the seven Spirits of God, the four creatures (representing the redeemed sons of God from the four corners of the earth), twenty-four elders (representing the ministers of God of Old and New Testament), angels, and Jesus, all of which will be part of the symbolic choreography of our past and future history. Jesus holds a scroll secured with seven seals, which He breaks one by one with different effects on earth. The first four out of the seven seals are characterized by the "Riders of the Apocalypse," representing the humble ministers of Jesus, who boldly went forth, in obedience to the divine command, to preach to the entire known world the gospel of Jesus Christ (represent the rider of the white horse); the Pagans, which are the great opposers of the establishment of Christianity that persecutes and kills them (represent the rider of the red horse); an apostate ministry, possessing power and authority to enforce the severest exactions upon the true church, producing a desolating spiritual famine (represent the rider of the black horse); the Popes often ordered crusades against peoples in which the sword, starvation, and every other means of cruelty imaginable were used to exterminate the so-called heresy (represent the rider of the pale horse). The fifth seal shows the souls of millions who lost their lives at the instigation of the Pagans, and later the apostate Church of Rome (Papal and Protestant) requesting to be vindicated of their righteous blood, but God asks them to wait for another great period of persecution to come. The sixth seal is about overthrown kingdoms, and their rulers and princes made objects of the most gloomy terror. It describes the continuous attacks by barbarian hordes from all directions, severely hurting Pagan Rome. Up to this point, the vision represents a synopsis of the whole book, containing the history of the church apostate to its final end and also the contemporaneous history of the true Church of God. The seventh seal details the account of the great persecuting powers, civil and ecclesiastical, and the trials and triumphs of the Church of God, developing more fully the events described under the sixth seal.

What follows are the seven angels, each successively sounding a trumpet, signaling the decline of the Western Roman Empire to its eventual fall. The first trumpet signals the attacks of Alaric and his Gothic hordes from the North that burst like a tornado upon the empire about the beginning of the 5th century, spreading destruction and desolation upon every side. They overran Italy, harassed or captured Rome repeatedly, and threatened to overthrow the empire, but made no permanent settlement in the territory. The second trumpet indicates the invasion of "the terrible Genseric" with his Vandal hordes, who pushed southward through

Gaul (France) and Spain, conquered the Carthaginian territory of northern Africa, and there formed a permanent independent government in AD 439. From this fixed position, Genseric began repetitive and desolating incursions onto the Roman Empire throughout the Mediterranean Sea. The third trumpet sounds the arrival of Attila and his Huns, who were even more cruel and barbarous than the Goths and the Vandals. They came from the remote solitudes of Asia and poured like a whirlwind, first upon the inhabitants of the Eastern empire (in AD 442 and 445) and then turned their attention westward. After his defeat at Chalons by the combined forces of the Visigoths, Alans, Franks, and Romans, Attila suddenly died in AD 453. The fourth trumpet summarizes the previous three as retributive justice to humble Pagan Rome for the slaughter of millions of Christians. The fifth trumpet signals the arrival of a religious impostor under Muhammad, who retired to a cave in Hera, near Mecca, and there received his pretended revelations in AD 606. His followers and warriors, the Saracens, made extensive conquests and gained immense numbers of converts. But they did not overthrow the Eastern empire, neither did they destroy the Roman church, corrupt and apostate as it was. The sixth trumpet marks the attacks of the Turks, which eventually became the Ottoman Empire, who first took possession of Armenia Major in the 9th century, where they increased in numbers, and in the space of two hundred years, became a formidable power. At the end of this period, they combined into four Sultanies, the heads of which were at Bagdad, Damascus, Aleppo, and Iconium between AD 1055 and 1080. Counting their first victory in Europe in AD 1281 and their last conquest in AD 1672 gives the exact timeline provided by the prophecy; 391 years and 15 days.

Just as there was a pause between the sixth and the seventh seal, there is a pause between the sixth and the seventh trumpet. An angel warns that when the seventh trumpet sounds, God's mysterious final plan will be fulfilled. John is asked to eat a small scroll handed to him, which is sweet to the taste but bitter in the stomach, signaling that the Word of God is taken eagerly and with gladness, but this is followed by bitter opposition and even persecution. Then there is the story of the two witnesses in sackcloth that will prophesy for 1,260 years. When the apostasy arose, the governing power of the Word and Spirit of God in the church was gradually usurped by the rising hierarchy of the Papal church, until men had entire authority. This Papal apostasy then eventually gave way to the Protestant apostasy. Since creed and sect-making first began, the Word and Spirit, the two witnesses referred to, have not possessed governing power and authority in Protestantism. "A vast number of the clergy no longer regard the Bible as the inspired Word of God to man, but simply as a remarkable piece of religious literature recording the natural development of the religious consciousness among a peculiarly sensitive race of people. While Protestants will not for a moment allow the blessed Book to be hidden out of sight, they will not grant it that place it should occupy as the sole discipline of faith."

What follows is a retracing a bit of the story. The Church of God, under the new covenant, will go through tribulations. Pagan Rome will engage in persecutions, torture, and death against Christian ministers, its followers, and its new converts. However, truth will prevail. Before this happens, though, the Roman beast will change from Pagan to Papal. The Reformation will hurt the Papacy, which almost disappeared in early and mid 19th century. Yet it is saved by Benito Mussolini with the creation in 1929 of the Vatican State. Protestantism, which is an imitation of the Papal original, by its adoption of a religious system with ecclesiastical power, share the mark of the beast. Their followers adopt the mark by believing in the religious system and the power they allow to be under. They accept the mark by essentially becoming accomplices of the sins of their religion. Things change when God writes His name on its chosen people, restoring the gospel of truth. "At about the year 1880, God began to raise up Holy men and women whom he commissioned to preach the everlasting gospel of the kingdom again. They preach, teach, and believe every word of truth placed in the Bible without a conference, organization, or discipline of men."

Again, the story is repeated under seven angels, each pouring a bowl to different places on earth, affecting it in different ways. The first bowl is poured on land, corrupting people's morals. The second bowl is poured on the sea, affecting the inhabitants by the slaughter and massacre that the French Revolution caused. The third bowl is poured on the rivers and springs, indicating the spreading of anti-monarchic sentiments originated in France throughout Europe. The fourth bowl is poured on the sun, signaling Napoleonic tyrant rule, bloody battles, and the rejection of God. The fifth bowl is poured on the beast's throne, signifying the downfall of the Papacy and the Holy Roman Empire. The sixth bowl is poured on the Euphrates River, indicating the source of the Ottoman Empire that for seven centuries became an active hindrance against the cause of Christ. The seventh bowl is poured into the air, affecting the entire world with a complete and final overthrow of all civil and ecclesiastical powers, which is still in the future.

What follows next consists of a number of distinct themes running over the ground already covered. Much like Babylon was "the center of the earth's idolatry and stood first of all as the direct enemy of God's people," it is represented as the false church being the center of earth's spiritual idolatry. There are other harlots or corrupt churches in the world besides her, but the Papacy is the mother of them all. They are all children by her side. Some of them greatly honor her and, in deep veneration, call her "our holy mother church," but God brands her as the "mother of harlots and abominations of the earth." This apostate church is "drunk with the blood of God's Holy people," meaning she is responsible for the persecution, torture, and death of witnesses for Jesus, the real Church of God.

The following events will take place in the future. After the resurrection of the Word and Spirit of God by the true church, a voice from heaven is heard (Rev, 11:12), "Then a loud voice from heaven called to the two prophets, 'Come up here!' And they rose to heaven in a cloud as their enemies watched." This ascension up to heaven in the presence of their enemies, which according to this chapter, will occur before the Tribulations of the end of times, Christians call it "the Rapture." The true Church of God will be "taken up" or raptured to heaven. Once the church is no longer on earth, evil is now able to act freely. Once evil is under this unrestricted condition, there will be a huge political upheaval in the world and great destruction. At the end, governments will be overthrown, and eventually, Jesus Christ will be the only king remaining. His mission will be to raise the dead so that they may be judged, to give reward to the prophets and true believers, and to banish with everlasting destruction those who corrupted the earth.

Conclusion

Because of our fallen human nature, our struggle between good and evil is translated into everything we think and do. Therefore, these fallen traits are found in politics and religion. In terms of politics, we have demonstrated that a system that allows us to develop with the least government restrictions, both economically and in terms of personal freedom, is the one that has provided the most stability and that has lifted from poverty the most people throughout our entire history. That system is irrefutably Capitalism under Libertarian or Free Market political philosophies. Communism is Socialism imposed to the citizenry by force. Socialism uses the democratic system to gain power, and once there, it strives to change the rules to stay in power even though the majority does not agree with their political philosophy. No country in the entire history of the world has improved the condition of its citizenry under either Communism or Socialism. How about China, you might ask? Well, China actually uses Capitalism to expand its economic power while maintaining its citizenry under tight communist control. It lures companies to set up shop in China, given its low overhead operational costs (low wages, low employee benefit liabilities, cheap land, ready or built to specifications infrastructure, etc.), in exchange for huge profits compared to setting up shop in any other country. Imagine the profits gained in this deal that the companies accept to sell up to 51% of their shares to the Chinese elite (the heads of the Chinese communist party) in order to operate in China. That is not the way Capitalism is designed to work. This is a complete bastardization of Capitalism. This is "globalist Socialism."

In terms of religion, we have shown that evil uses religion to stray us away from God's truth. Even during apparent good things that occurred in history, such as the Roman empire finally adopting Christianity as its official religion after 300 years of persecution, torture, and murder of the true church, evil concocted a system that bastardized Christianity with Roman Paganism to create the Papacy, which ended up being as ugly and murderous as the previous system of religion. Satan is known as "the father of lies" and, as such, has distorted the truth from the beginning of time. In the past, his lies were spread to people through religion, a false belief system based on human ambition for wealth and power, which enslaved people with rituals to disguise evil with spirituality. This mix of politics and religion is incarnated first by the Papacy and later by Protestantism in Europe; and Mohammedanism, Hinduism, and Buddhism in most of the rest of the world. A variation of this characteristic can be seen in communist and socialist countries, where the forced cult of the state replaces religion. We have also touched on the "new Socialism" embodied by Globalism, in which "the world" is the new cult forced upon everyone. In this respect, evil, disguised in religion, the cult of the state, or of the things of this world, seeks to spread across the planet, not so much through tradition and oppression, as it used to be, but through all available systems of communication that technology avails. Fake news has always existed; it is just so much more apparent now for those who can see through the evil political intentions. For those who had "the scales fallen from their eyes" and now can see clearly, it is just amazing to hear those who are still blinded, defend those lies and even attack those who try to show them the facts that prove them wrong. There is nothing left but to pray for them and keep pointing at the truth each available opportunity with the peace of mind that at the end, Truth will prevail.

To conclude, I take refuge in Jesus' following exhortation at the conclusion of the book of Revelation (Rev. 22:11-15): "Let the one who is doing harm continue to do harm, let the one who is vile continue to be vile, let the one who is righteous continue to live righteously, let the one who is holy continue to be holy. Look, I am coming soon, bringing my reward with me to repay all people according to their deeds. I am the Alpha and the Omega, the First and the Last, the Beginning and the End. Blessed are those who wash their robes. They will be permitted to enter through the gates of the city and eat the fruit from the tree of life. Outside the city are the dogs, the sorcerers, the sexually immoral, the murderers, the idol worshipers, and all who love to live a lie." Amen to that!

Testimony

I was a sinner who needed a Savior. I am still a sinner, but now I know who my Savior is, how He saved me, and why. This is my story.

I loved the sciences but always had problems with math until sixth grade when a new teacher, who had the reputation of being severe, explained the mathematical process in a way that made sense to me. This made me realize that I really did not have a problem understanding math, but had a problem with the way it was normally taught. From that moment on, I went from a kid who always had bad grades in math, to obtaining degrees in oceanography, environmental sciences, and civil engineering. As a man of science, my concept of God was abstract. My Catholic upbringing gave me the notion of the Holy Trinity, but I really did not know what it meant. I was never atheistic or skeptic, but certainly, a scientist, whatever that means. I say this because I later battled with the idea of creation and the wonderful things of creation, all microscopic, macroscopic, and astronomic. The order, the perfection, the details, the purpose for all things, and how everything has a function. This cannot be the product of chance. The wonderful design of all things must have a Designer, a Creator, and a Conductor. If this is so, things of God and science must be connected because God also created the laws upon which science is built. There is no other explanation.

I was your typical sinner who thought of himself as being a good person, that is; my good deeds surely outweighed my bad ones, and since I was not a murderer, a liar, a drunkard, etc., I should be OK in the eyes of God. Then I had the urge to look into the Bible, not so much to learn the "Word of God," but as a research exercise to see if there were contradictions. I wanted to compare the different Gospels. To my surprise, the Bible has references to all other part of the book, so the work was already done. There was nothing hidden to be discovered. Then I stumbled on a Christian radio station that had programs with several pastors discussing and expounding on the life of Christ and the stories of the Bible. I had to travel long distances for my job, so the radio was a good companion. Pretty soon, I made a point to listen to the programs even when I was not traveling and listened to it during my lunch breaks. I did this for a couple of years. Listening and learning; how the Bible was His Story centered in Jesus Christ, how it was written by men but inspired by the Holy Spirit evidenced by the number of fulfilled prophesies of His first coming and even more prophesies of His second coming, among many other things.

On one of these lunch breaks, I decided to say the Believer's Prayer, and my entire being changed forever. Not only were my eyes opened even wider than they already were, but my mind was blown away with the jolt that the Holy Spirit produced in me as I invited Him to take over my life. I began to see, think, and react to things differently. I recited the Scriptures that I barely knew before. I understood the reason for the progression of things described in the Bible. People around me, out of the blue, began to ask me about spiritual matters, and surprisingly, I had answers. But I was not happy with the little I knew about the Bible, so I began to read it all from the beginning. The first time I read it, I devoured it. As I was reading it, I could identify all kind of gems in its pages. The second time I read it, I decided to flag out these gems in five different categories: Christophanies (the occasions when Jesus appeared in the Old Testament times), prayers, predictions about Jesus, predictions about the future, and instructions. Every time I read it again, I discovered more and more hidden gems. With time, I was compelled to write in my own words commentaries of various subjects. Maybe I can return the favor to my math teacher by explaining my understanding of the Truth in a way other people can understand it. This culminated with publishing this book. Skeptics can react to these words with the same attitude as Pilates when he asked Jesus: "What is Truth?", but he did not wait for His answer. Well, Truth is the manifestation of reality as perceived not by you but by God. This is the theme of the book.

Acknowledgement

To my wife Rocio, the mother of our children, my lover, and my best friend. Without your love and support, I would have not been able to accomplish this.

References

(All the websites listed here were accurate at the time of publication, but they can change in the future, even disappear.)

Gallup
https://news.gallup.com/poll/1663/media-use-evaluation.aspx

"Economic Justice." The Movement for Black Lives. Accessed September 11, 2017. https://policy.m4bl.org/economic-justice/. Archive: https://www.influencewatch.org/app/uploads/2017/08/The-Movement-for-Black-Lives-M4BL-Economic-Justice.pdf ^

International Monetary Fund
https://data.imf.org/?sk=4FFB52B2-3653-409A-B471-D47B46D904B5&sId=1485878708037

Trading Economics
www.tradingeconomics.com

The CATO Institute
https://www.cato.org/human-freedom-index-new

Migration Policy Institute
https://www.migrationpolicy.org/programs/data-hub/charts/top-25-destinations-international-migrants?width=1000&height=850&iframe=true

Federation for American Immigration Reform
https://www.fraserinstitute.org/sites/default/files/
ProductivityProsperityBusinessTaxes.pdf

McIntyre, S. & McKitrick, R. (2003) Corrections to the Mann
et al. (1998) proxy database and northern hemispheric average
temperature series. Energy & the Environment. Volume 14, No. 6.
pp. 751-771.
https://climateaudit.files.wordpress.com/2005/09/mcintyre.
mckitrick.2003.pdf

The 8 Beliefs You Should Know about Mormons When They
Knock at the Door
https://www.thegospelcoalition.org/blogs/justin-taylor/the-8-
beliefs-you-should-know-about-mormons-when-they-knock-at-
the-door/

Wikipedia. 2021. "Book of Mormon." Last Modified Date: 9 March
2021. https://en.wikipedia.org/wiki/Book_of_Mormon

Islam
https://www.history.com/topics/religion/islam

Wikipedia. 2021. "Quran." Last Modified Date: 1 March 2021.
https://en.wikipedia.org/wiki/Quran

Core Beliefs of Hindus
https://www.dummies.com/religion/hinduism/core-beliefs-of-
hindus/

Wikipedia. 2021. "Vedas." Last Modified Date: 6 February 2021.
https://en.wikipedia.org/wiki/Vedas

Judaism
https://www.history.com/topics/religion/judaism#section_3

Christianity
https://www.history.com/topics/religion/history-of-christianity

Wikipedia. 2021. "Bible." Last Modified Date: 7 March 2021.
https://en.wikipedia.org/wiki/Bible

Frederick George Smith. Second Ed. 1918. "The Revelation
Explained, An Exposition, Text by Text, of the Apocalypse of
St. John." Project Gutenberg. 2004. http://www.gutenberg.org/
ebooks/13229

Bible quotes in New Living Translation (NLT) and New King James
(NKJ) versions. 2021. Bible Gateway. https://www.biblegateway.
com/quicksearch/?quicksearch=Genesis&version=NLT